Meaning and the Moral Sciences

*International Library of Philosophy
and Scientific Method*

Editor: Ted Honderich

A catalogue of books already published in the
International Library of Philosophy and Scientific Method
will be found at the end of this volume

Meaning and the Moral Sciences

Hilary Putnam

*Professor of Philosophy and
Walter Beverley Pearson Professor
of Modern Mathematics and
Mathematical Logic,
Harvard University*

London, Henley and Boston

ROUTLEDGE & KEGAN PAUL

First published in 1978
by Routledge & Kegan Paul Ltd
39 Store Street,
London WC1E 7DD,
Broadway House,
Newtown Road,
Henley-on-Thames,
Oxon RG9 1EN and
9 Park Street,
Boston, Mass. 02108, USA
Set in 11 on 12 Garamond
by Kelly and Wright, Bradford-on-Avon, Wiltshire
and printed in Great Britain by
Lowe & Brydone Ltd.

British Library Cataloguing in Publication Data

Putnam, Hilary

Meaning and the moral sciences.—(International
library of philosophy and scientific mothod).
1. Meaning (Philosophy)
I. Title   II. Series
149' .94   B105.M4   77–30433

ISBN 0 7100 8754 3

CONTENTS

PREFACE

The lectures that make up this volume were written during a period of two years that were extraordinarily eventful years for me. The invitation to give the John Locke Lectures at Oxford University in 1976 combined with the fortunate accident of my having a sabbatical year due from Harvard University to give me both the time and the stimulus for prolonged writing. The Locke Lectures grew out of reflections stimulated by Hartry Field's provocative article on Tarski's theory of truth. As the first draft flowed from my pen I was amazed at the conclusions I found myself coming to (e.g. that there is something to Quine's 'indeterminacy of translation' thesis) and pleased that I could connect my interest in the epistemology of ethics (which is at a very preliminary and undeveloped stage, I must hasten to add) with my dissatisfaction with what I call 'scientific utopianism' in the lectures. Still, when I arrived at Oxford with six lectures to give in the (happily named) Hilary term of 1976, I had only the first drafts of four or five with me. Somehow I managed to finish them without ever actually showing up for a lecture unprepared, and I know that the peace, the stimulation, and the warmth of the Oxford atmosphere helped me to work with intensity.

So many people showed me kindness and friendship during that brief stay that I could not begin to mention all their names (nor would a list be likely to be of general interest). But I must add that the opportunity to give the Shearman Lectures at the University of London gave me the excuse to see a good deal of my friends in London, and that this stimulation (social as well as philosophical) was important to me, and that the talks I had with friends in Cambridge left me with questions to brood about for many months afterwards.

I also want to say that being John Locke Professor was not only an honour, but for an anglophile and a Zuleika Dobson fan like myself, a splendid opportunity to fulfil a great many donnish fantasies. In particular, living in University College was an experience I shall always cherish (and I *have* to mention George Cawkwell, who did so much to ease the culture shock and to make me feel at home). That winter was the winter of the drought (although we didn't yet realize it was a drought), so there was no rain or snow, and spring came early – by mid-February. So there were marvellous opportunities for looking at the architecture of Oxford, for weekends in the country, and so forth.

After Oxford, I went to Israel, which I had never seen, so once again there was the danger of culture shock happily averted by the help of warm friends (I have to mention Yehuda Elkana) and the beauty of the country and of Jerusalem. Since the University of Jerusalem sponsored an international conference on philosophy of language at that time (unfortunately, Yehoshua Bar Hillel died earlier in the year, so that his contribution to the conference was prevented) this was also a time to see more of Peter Strawson and of Michael Dummett.

Since I had missed most of Dummett's William James Lectures (which took place at Harvard while I was at Oxford), I was delighted that he could come to Jerusalem and that he commented on 'Reference and Understanding', which was in large part a reaction to the William James Lectures (to the ones I heard and to the typescript of the others). His comments were very important for my thinking, and while there are still many points of disagreement in our views, the turn in my thinking represented by 'Realism and Reason' is, in part, the result of our dialogue.

'Realism and Reason' was, however, not written in the sabbatical year, but rather during the fall of 1976. And the most important event of that fall for my work was Nelson Goodman's suggestion that he and Willard van Quine and I do a series of three joint meetings of our seminars at which we would discuss each other's views. I knew that I found these three 'shows' (as the graduate students irreverently called them) tremendously stimulating, and that this intense interaction with Goodman's views (as well as with Quine's – however the influence of Quine's thought on my work is of long standing) also shaped 'Realism and Reason'.

I trust that I have given the impression that I had a good time while I was writing these lectures. I hope the reader will have a good time reading them.

And, of course, my gratitude to the National Endowment for the Humanities for making it all possible.

INTRODUCTION

Before Kant almost every philosopher subscribed to the view that truth is some kind of correspondence between ideas and 'what is the case'. However puzzling the *nature* of the 'correspondence' may be, the naturalness of the idea is undeniable. There is a world out there; and what we say or think is 'true' when it *gets it the way it is* and 'false' when it doesn't correspond to *the way it is*.

With Kant a new view emerges: the view that truth is radically mind-dependent. It is not that the thinking mind *makes up* the world on Kant's view; but it doesn't just mirror it either.

To the present time, views of truth can be divided into two kinds: 'realist' views, which interpret truth as some kind of correspondence to what is the case, and 'verificationist' views, which interpret truth as, for example, what would be *verified* under ideal conditions of inquiry. (I choose Peirce's form as my example of a verificationist view because it seems to me the most tenable; but, of course, there are many versions of both the realist view and the verificationist view in the literature.)

In the early decades of the twentieth century, there were many philosophers of an empiricist stamp who held neither sort of view, however. These philosophers *rejected* the whole notion of 'truth' as 'metaphysical'. (An example is John Dewey, who always spoke of 'warranted assertibility', and not of 'truth'.) In particular, many of the Vienna positivists shared this attitude of suspicious hostility toward the concept of truth until the work of Alfred Tarski.

The reader will find an account of Tarski's work in the first Lecture in this volume; what is important is that this work was taken by the philosophers to be *deflationary*. What Tarski does is show how, in the context of a formalized language, one can define 'true' (or a predicate which can be used in place of 'true') using *only* the notions of the object language and notions of pure mathematics. In particular, no semantical notion – no such notion as 'designates', or 'stands for', or 'refers to' – is taken as primitive by Tarski (although 'refers to' gets *defined* – defined in terms of non-semantical notions – in the course of his work). Thus anyone who accepts the notions of whatever object language is in question – and this can be chosen arbitrarily – can also understand 'true' as defined by Tarski for that object language. 'True' is just as legitimate as any notion of first order science.

What is essential is that Tarski verifies the correctness of his 'truth-definition' in any particular case by seeing that it satisfies a certain equivalence condition. This condition is that to say of any sentence that the sentence is true must be equivalent (in fact, Tarski requires it to be *provably* equivalent) to the sentence itself. To use Tarski's famous example, if 'Snow is white' is a sentence of the object language, then 'true' must be so defined (for that object language) that it becomes provable (in the language in which the definition is given – Tarski calls this latter the *meta-language*) that

'Snow is white' is true if and only if snow is white.

An example of the use that empiricist philosophers made of this is the following: a minor pragmatist called Felix Kaufmann had argued that 'true' is a metaphysical' notion ('metaphysical' being a pejorative word) on the ground that (he alleged that) ascriptions of the predicate 'true' could never be verified or falsified. We can tell if a statement is *confirmed* to a given degree, Kaufmann said, but since *perfect* confirmation is impossible, we have never verified that the statement is absolutely *true*. Carnap, relying on Tarski's work, replied to Kaufmann as follows: liberal empiricists (including Kaufmann himself) do not require that ascriptions of a predicate be verifiable with certainty in order that the predicate be allowed into an empiricist language. For example, we can test with probability high enough for all practical (and even scientific) purposes whether or not current flows through a wire; so the predicate 'is such that current is flowing', as a predicate applied to copper wires, is accepted as empirically meaningful. But if

'Current is flowing through this wire'

has a probability, say, of 0·999 then the meta-language sentence

'Current is flowing through this wire' is true

has exactly the same probability of 0·999 by the equivalence condition. Kaufmann is right that it is not *verifiable with certainty* that the sentence '"Current is flowing through this wire" is true' is correct, but it is *verifiable with probability*, namely, by verifying the corresponding object-language sentence 'Current is flowing through this wire', and using the equivalence condition.

Thus it happened that by the 1930s Carnap, Popper, Hempel, etc., all accepted the notion 'true' as a notion that even the most scrupulous empiricist could be happy with. But they accepted it *because they thought that it did no philosophical work*. Indeed, if one identifies the correspondence theory of truth with the equivalence condition, then the correspondence theory of truth likewise does no philosophical work. That '*Snow is white*' *is true if and only if snow is white* is just a tautology. This tautology tells us nothing about how 'Snow is white' is *used* or *understood*, nothing about its assertibility, etc.

Not surprisingly, there was soon a realist reaction to the claim that theory of truth is philosophically uninteresting (and the notion of truth itself philosophically neutral). In a paper I read to the undergraduate philosophy club at Oxford University in 1960 which I titled 'Do true assertions correspond to reality?' I wrote

> I want to explore the question: whether any sense can
> be made of the traditional view that a true assertion is one
> that corresponds to reality. Two opinions seem to be
> widespread: (a) that some sense *can* be made of the view,
> and that some sense *is* made of it (as much as can be hoped
> for) by Tarski's 'semantical conception of truth';
> (b) that the view collapses as soon as one asks searching
> questions about the nature of the alleged 'correspondence'.
> I shall try to show that both of these opinions are incorrect.

The strategy I followed, and that has since been followed by a number of philosophers, is to view the language-speaker as constructing a symbolic representation of his environment. He cannot do this unless he causally interacts with his environment, and the accuracy or inaccuracy of his representation will affect the viability and success of his efforts in dealing with his environment; thus such an account of the relation of language-speakers to the world is part of a causal model of human behaviour. In so far as the assumed correspondence between the representations in the speaker's mind and their external referents is part of the model, realism thus becomes an *empirical hypothesis*. In an essay included in this volume ('Reference and Understanding') I attempt to spell out this sort of view and contrast it with other views. The reader will also find discussion of the idea that realism is an empirical hypothesis, and of the work of Richard Boyd, who has advanced a related view, in the second of my Locke Lectures in this volume.

The strategy, it should be said, is not to show that Tarski is *wrong*. Rather, the argument is that what Tarski has done is to give us a perfectly correct account of the formal logic of the concept 'true'. But the formal logic of the concept is not all there is to the notion of truth. Tarski's work requires supplementation; and when this philosophical supplementation is provided, we see that the notion of truth is not philosophically neutral, and that a correspondence account is needed to understand how language works and how science works.

In the early 1970s an extraordinarily brilliant and provocative article ('Tarski's Theory of Truth') by Hartry Field appeared, which did contain a serious attack on Tarski's work from a realist perspective, however. Field argued that precisely that part of Tarski's work that exploits the equivalence condition is unsatisfactory, and that this part of Tarski's work must be replaced by a different sort of theory if we are to have scientifically respectable standards in the theory of language.

Although I could not agree with Field's conclusion, I regarded this article as posing a profound issue for discussion, and my Locke Lectures were originally conceived as a detailed examination of precisely the issue raised by Field; the issue of trying to find (or demanding that we seek) a 'physicalistic' theory of reference, i.e. a theory that says that a speaker refers to some thing when he uses a term just in case his use of that term stands in a definite causal relation (to be defined by empirical science, in just the spirit that empirical science has 'defined' *water* as H_2O and *temperature* as mean molecular kinetic energy) to that something, or to things of the same kind as that something (in a sense of 'same kind' which would also have to be defined). What I did not foresee is that in the course of discussing (and explaining my reasons for rejecting) Field's criticism of Tarski, I would be led into a discussion of the issue of scientism in the social sciences, as represented by Mill's celebrated dictum that 'the backward state of the Moral Sciences' can only be remedied by imitating the methods of physics. The reader will find that the Locke Lectures gradually move from a specific discussion of the notions of truth and reference to questions which have to do with the character of linguistic inquiry in general and even of social scientific inquiry in general.

I have included in the present volume one essay on moral and literary topics, in spite of the sketchiness which it exhibits, because I want to make explicit a connection which I believe exists between the mistaken view that I think we have of the social sciences and the mistaken view – it amounts to a major cultural phenomenon – known as the 'fact/value distinction'. The connection resides in the presumption that the words 'truth' and 'knowledge' are somehow the *property* of 'science' (construed on a particular model). I think that Aristotle was profoundly right in holding that ethics is concerned with how to live and with human happiness, and also profoundly right in holding that this sort of *knowledge* ('practical knowledge') is different from theoretical knowledge. A view of knowledge that acknowledges that the sphere of knowledge is wider than the sphere of 'science' seems to me to be a cultural necessity if we are to arrive at a sane and human view of ourselves *or* of science.

The final essay in this volume represents a recent turn in my thinking. Broadly speaking, the thrust is that a 'verificationist' view of truth and a correspondence theory of truth (in the sense of empirical realism) are *not* incompatible. Inasmuch as Kant had a view which included a correspondence view of truth *within* the empirical realm (on my reading, anyway) *and* a stress on the mind-dependence of all truth, there is (I like to think) something Kantian in the view with which I end up. But it is a demythologized Kantianism, without 'things in themselves' and 'transcendental egos'.

These essays cover a number of different topics, obviously. But (except for 'Science, Literature, and Reflection') they were written within a two-year period, and are all intimately connected. The fact is that the great metaphysical problem of realism, the nature of language and reference, and the character of our knowledge of ourselves and our knowledge *are* topics that overlap, interrelate, and inform one another. I hope the reader will end this book convinced that this is the case.

PART ONE

MEANING AND KNOWLEDGE

(The John Locke Lectures, 1976)

LECTURE I

The nature of truth is a very ancient problem in philosophy; but not until the present century did philosophers and logicians attempt to separate this problem from the problems of the nature of knowledge and the nature of warranted belief. That one could have a theory of truth which is neutral with respect to epistemological questions, and even with respect to the great metaphysical issue of realism versus idealism, would have seemed preposterous to a nineteenth-century philosopher. Yet that is just what the most prestigious theory of truth, Tarski's theory,[1] claims to be.

Although it requires a certain amount of sophisticated logic to present this theory properly, one of the leading ideas, the idea of 'disquotation', is easy to explain. Take any sentence – say, *Snow is white*. Put quotation marks around that sentence – thus:

'Snow is white.'

Now adjoin the words 'is true' – thus:

'Snow is white' is true.

The resulting sentence is itself one which is true if and only if the original sentence is true. It is, moreover, *assertible* if and only if the original sentence is assertible; it is probable to degree r if and only if the original sentence is probable to degree r; etc. According to Tarski, Carnap, Quine, Ayer, and similar theorists, knowing these facts is the key to understanding the words 'is true'. In short, to understand *P is true*, where P is a sentence in quotes, just 'disquote' P – take off the quotation marks (and erase 'is true').

E.g. what does

'Snow is white' is true

mean? It means

Snow is white

What does

'There is a real external world' is true

mean? It means

There is a real external world

And so on.

The claim that 'disquotation' theorists are advancing is that an answer to the question *what does it mean to say* that something is true need not commit itself to a view about what that something in turn means or about how that something is or is not to be verified. You can have a materialist interpretation of 'Snow is white'; you can believe 'Snow is white' is verifiable, or that it is only falsifiable but not verifiable; or that it is only confirmable to a degree between zero and one; or none of the foregoing; but 'Snow is white' is still equi-assertible with '"Snow is white" is true'. On this view, 'true' is, amazingly, a *philosophically neutral* notion. 'True' is just a device for 'semantic ascent' – for 'raising' assertions from the 'object language' to the 'meta-language', and the device does not commit one epistemologically or meta-physically.

I shall now sketch the second leading idea of Tarski's theory. 'True' is a predicate of sentences in Tarski's theory; and these sentences have to be in some formalized language L, if the theory is to be made precise. (How to extend the theory to natural languages is today a great topic of concern among philosophers and linguists.) Now a 'language' in this sense has a *finite* number of undefined or 'primitive' predicates. For simplicity, let us suppose our language L has only two primitive predicates – 'is the moon' and 'is blue'. For predicates P, the locution

P refers to x

whose intimate connection with the word 'true' can be brought out by using the phrase 'is true of' instead of 'refers to', thus:

P is true of x

can also be explained by employing the idea of disquotation: if P is the predicate 'is the moon' we have:

'Is the moon' refers to x if and only if x is the moon.

And if P is the predicate 'is blue' we have:

'Is blue' refers to x if and only if x is blue.

So the 'meta-linguistic' predication:

'Is the moon' refers to x

is equivalent to the 'object-language' predication:

x is the moon

Let us say P *primitively refers* to x if P is a primitive predicate (in the case of our language L, 'is the moon' or 'is blue') and P refers to x. Then *primitive reference* can be defined *for our particular example L* by giving a list:

Definition:
P primitively refers to x if and only if (1) P is the phrase 'is the moon' and x is the moon, or (2) P is the phrase 'is blue' and x is blue.

And for any *particular formalized language* a similar definition of primitive reference can be given, once we have been given a list of the primitive predicates of that language.

The rest of Tarski's idea requires logic and mathematics to explain properly. I shall be *very* sketchy now.

The non-primitive predicates of a language are built up out of primitive ones by various devices – truth functions and quantifiers. Suppose, for the sake of an example, that the only devices are disjunction and negation: forming the predicates 'P *or* Q', and '*not*-P' from the predicate P. Then we define reference as follows:

(I) If P contains zero logical connectives, *P refers to x* if and only if P primitively refers to x.
(II) P *or* Q *refers to x* if P refers to x or Q refers to x.

(III) *Not*-P *refers to* x if P does not refer to x.

Turning this inductive definition[2] into a proper definition is where much of the technical logic comes in; suffice it to say this can be done. The result is a definition of 'reference' *for a particular language* – a *definition which uses no semantical words* (no words in the same family as 'true' and 'refers').

Finally, supposing that our simple language is so simple[3] that all sentences are of the forms *for every* x, Px, *for some* x, Px, or truth-functions of these (where P is a predicate), then *true* would be defined as follows (of course, Tarski actually considered much richer languages):

   (I) *for every* x, Px is *true* if and only if, for every x, P refers to x.

  (II) *for some* x, Px is *true* if and only if, for some x, P refers to x.

 (III) if *p* and *q* are sentences, *p or q* is *true* if *p* is true or *q* is true; and *not*-p is true if *p* is not true.

While I have left out the mathematics of Tarski's work (how one turns an 'inductive definition' like the above into an 'explicit' definition of the form 'something is true if and only if . . .', where 'true' and 'refers' do not occur in '. . .') and I have ignored the immense complications which arise when the language has *relations* – two-place (or three-place, etc.) predicates – I hope I have conveyed three ideas:

  (1) 'Truth' and 'reference' are defined *for one particular language at a time*. We are not defining the relation 'true in L' for *arbitrary* L.

  (2) Primitive reference is defined 'by a list'; and reference and truth in general are defined by induction on the number of logical connectives in the predicate or sentence, starting with primitive reference.

  (3) The 'inductive' definition by a system of clauses such as (I), (II), (III), (I'), (II'), (III'), can be turned into a *bona fide* 'explicit definition' by technical devices from logic.

As a check on the correctness of what has been done, it is easy to derive the following theorem from the definition of 'true':

'*For some* x, x *is the moon*' is *true* if and only if, for
some x, x is the moon.

And in fact, one can derive from the definition of true that

(T) 'P' is true if and only if P

when the dummy letter 'P' is replaced by any sentence of our
language L.

That this should be the case – that the above schema (T) be
one all of whose instances are consequences of the definition
of 'true' – is Tarski's 'Criterion of Adequacy' (the famous
'Criterion T') for definitions of 'is true'.

Notice that while the idea of disquotation may initially strike
one as trivial, Tarski's theory is obviously very non-trivial. The
reason is that the idea of disquotation only tells us that the
Criterion T is correct; but it does not tell us how to define 'true'
so that the Criterion T will be satisfied. Nor does disquotation
by itself enable us to eliminate 'true' from all the contexts in
which it occurs. '*Snow is white*' *is true* is equivalent to *Snow is
white*; but to what sentence *not containing the word 'true'* (or any
other 'semantical' term) is the following sentence equivalent:
*If the premises in an inference of the form p or q, not-p/∴q are both
true in L the conclusion is also true in L*? Tarski's method gives us an
equivalent for *this* sentence, and for other sentences in which
'is true' occurs with variables and quantifiers, and that is what
disquotation by itself does not do.

There are many problems with Tarski's theory which bothered
me for a number of years. One problem, which does *not* seem to
me to be too serious, is that 'true' is taken as a predicate of
sentences (i.e. strings of written signs) – strictly speaking, what
is being analysed is not 'is true', as a predicate of statements,
but 'expresses a true statement'. But I take it that, although it *is*
contrary to ordinary usage to speak of sentences as true or false,
this usage is perfectly clear, and also this amount of deviation
from ordinary usage is probably inevitable in *any* reconstruction
(e.g. the use of the word 'statement').[4] A more important objection is that the theory does not allow for sentences which are
neither true nor false (e.g. 'The number of trees in Canada is
even'), or sentences containing indexical words (such as 'now',
'here', 'I'). In fact, the theory can only be applied in its canonical
form to languages in which every predicate is well defined and

non-indexical. It now seems to me that it can be modified to apply to languages of other sorts; but this is not the sort of problem I shall deal with in these lectures. I shall also not distinguish between Tarski's original theory and a recent and very elegant variant proposed by Saul Kripke. The criticism I wish to deal with in detail – one with which I at one time agreed – is due to Hartry Field.[5]

Field concedes that Tarski did accomplish something of philosophical importance in showing how to define the semantical notions of reference and truth in terms of the semantical notion of primitive reference. But Tarski was wrong, Field contends, in thinking that he had philosophically clarified primitive reference. Here is the crucial paragraph from Field's article:[6]

> Now, it would have been easy for a chemist late in the last century, to have given a 'valence definition' of the following form:
>
> (3) $(\forall E) (\forall n)$ (E has valence n = E is potassium and n is $+1$, or . . . or E is sulphur and n is -2)
>
> where in the blanks go a list of similar clauses, one for each element. But, though this is an extensionally correct definition of valence, it would not have been an acceptable reduction; and had it turned out that nothing else was possible – had all efforts to explain valence in terms of the structural properties of atoms proved futile – scientists would have eventually had to decide either (a) to give up valence theory, or else (b) to replace the hypothesis of physicalism by another hypothesis (chemicalism?). It is part of scientific methodology to resist doing (a) as long as the notion of valence is serving the purposes for which it was designed (i.e., as long as it is proving useful in helping us characterize chemical compounds in terms of their valences). But the methodology is not to resist (a) and (b) by giving lists like (3); the methodology is to look for a real reduction. This is a methodology that has proved extremely fruitful in science, and I think we are giving up this fruitful methodology, unless we realize that we need to add theories of primitive reference to T_1 or T_2 if we are to establish the notion of truth as a physicalistically acceptable notion.

Lecture I

What Field contends is that the Tarski definition of *primitive reference* (in our example, P primitively refers to x if P is the phrase 'is the moon' and x is the moon or P is the phrase 'is blue' and x is blue) is exactly like the 'crazy valence definition' (3). In short, Field says we have *low standards* in theory of language; and we ought to have the same ('physicalistic') standards that we have in other natural sciences, especially if, as good physicalists, we view language as a natural phenomenon.

I find this fascinating because it illuminates an issue that has been submerged in philosophy for a long time, and that has surfaced in the twentieth century. Is *reference* just a relation between one thing, which happens to be a word (say, 'Mond') or a particular event of that word's being uttered, and another thing (say, the moon)? If so, is it a relation which is just as much part of the natural–casual order as the relation 'is chemically bonded to'? Is it to be studied in the same way? If not, are we viewing language as something transcendental (either in the Kantian or some other sense)? Or should we stop talking of 'reference' altogether? Field opts for the strong 'physicalist' view that answers 'yes' to my first three questions; even if he is wrong, that is what makes this paper so important and interesting.

I want to consider an ingenious (unpublished) reply to Field by Stephen Leeds. Leeds asks, in effect, what do we want a notion of truth *for*? For the purposes of deductive logic, e.g. to say 'in inferences of kind X, the conclusion is true whenever the premises are'. In expressing agreement, when we don't know exactly what sentence was uttered ('what he said was true'), etc.

Now, the following is Leeds's very neat observation: If we had a meta-language with *infinite conjunctions* and *infinite disjunctions* (countably infinite) we wouldn't need 'true'! If we wanted to say 'what he said was true', for example, we could say:

(1) [He said 'P_1' & P_1] or [He said 'P_2' & P_2] or . . .

where the disjunction in (1) contains one disjunct for each sentence 'P_i' of the object language.

But we *can't*, as a matter of fact, speak in infinite disjunctions. So instead we look for a finite expression equivalent to (1). Now,

(2) *For some* x *he said* x & x *is true*

will be equivalent to (1) provided for each i (i = 1, 2, 3, . . .)

(3) 'P$_i$' is true if and only if P$_i$

is correct. But this is just Tarski's 'Criterion T' – the famous Criterion of Adequacy. In short, any definition of 'true' is all right, *provided* (3) is satisfied. And it doesn't matter *what* the definition of 'true' looks like – it can be in terms of 'primitive reference' where 'primitive reference' is defined by a *list* in analogy to Field's 'crazy valence definition' – for, provided we *accept* (3) (i.e. accept all instances of (3)), then we know how to express all the infinite disjunctions we can't say by finite expressions we *can* say (on the model of expressing (1) by saying (2)).

The real point of Leeds's reply to Field is this: valence is an *explanatory* notion (i.e. a *causal-explanatory* notion). Since we intend the existence of various valences to figure in chemistry as a *cause*, we have to say what valence *is*, not just give the numerical values. But Leeds is *denying* that *reference* is a causal-explanatory notion. We need notions like truth and reference to *express* certain things (which could, in principle, be expressed in other ways – by using infinitary languages). For *this* purpose, it is *immaterial* if primitive reference is defined in what Field calls a 'crazy' way. Reference isn't (or, anyway, Field hasn't shown that it is) a causal-explanatory notion. In short, we can give a 'trans-cendental argument' for Tarski's procedure by appealing to a *purpose* for having notions like *truth* and *reference* which is not at all parallel to the purpose for which we have notions like *valence*.

One might object that Leeds is going to run into trouble with truth in the *meta*-language. But the same procedure works, except that the meta-language has to have *longer* – < $_2$ – infinite truth-functions. Anyway, the cute point about infinitary languages isn't really essential to Leeds's argument. What is essential is to justify Criterion T by pointing to a reason – other than causal explanation – for having notions like *truth* and *reference* in the language, and showing that satisfaction of Criterion T does the trick.

A deeper problem with Leeds's argument is this: what do we do about utterances like

(4) What he said was true

when the 'he' referred to wasn't speaking our object language? A natural line to take is this: the notion of reference *only* makes sense where the notion of translation makes sense. If we can't translate what 'he' was saying *at all* (of course, the translation doesn't have to capture every nuance to enable us to truth-value what was said, in most cases), how can we *understand* such an utterance as (4)?

This suggests the following idea: think of reference as defined *first* for the home language *à la* Tarski, and then extended to other languages *via* translation. Field, on the other hand, would contend that if I am referring to X that means (or consists in, or perhaps is empirically reducible to – in the 'water is H_2O' sense of empirical reduction) that I stand in a certain 'physicalistic' relation to X, tentatively the relation of being connected to X, or some property X has, by a certain kind of causal chain (to be specified!). And if 'he' is referring to X, no matter what language 'he' speaks, he is in the same physicalistic relation to X. So what it *means* for him to be *referring* to X *must* be explicated without referring to *my* language, and without employing the concept of *translation*. But why? Obviously, we can justify mapping other people's languages onto our own *without* assuming the existence of a unitary (let alone a 'physicalistic') relation of reference between words and things: mapping alien languages onto familiar ones (where possible) is a way of *rationalizing* other people's behaviour, and thereby facilitating dealings with them, predicting their behaviour, etc.

And if we are justified (by Leeds's argument) in having a notion of reference for our own language (a 'parochial' notion of reference, as Quine would say), we are justified in extending it to whatever languages we map onto our own language, in accordance with the mapping we employ.

Now, none of this shows that Field is wrong. It *could* be that there is a physicalistic relation of the kind Field has in mind between a word in L (where 'L' is a *variable* over natural languages) and whatever x it refers to, notwithstanding the fact that we don't need to assume or believe this to justify introducing such expressions as 'true' and 'refers' into our language. But the burden of proof seems to be very much on Field.

On the other hand, it seems to me that it is not *wholly* wrong to think of reference as a causal-explanatory notion. In the next lecture I am going to start spinning out an account which does justice to this realist intuition.

LECTURE II[*]

While it is undoubtedly a good thing that 'ism' words have gone out of fashion in philosophy, *some* 'ism' words seem remarkably resistant to being banned. One such word is 'realism'. More and more philosophers are talking about realism these days; but very little is said about what realism is.

Whatever else realists say, they typically say that they believe in a 'correspondence theory of truth'.

When they argue *for* their position, realists typically argue *against* some version of idealism – in our time, this would be positivism or operationalism. (This is not in itself surprising – all philosophers attempt to shift the burden of proof to their opponents. And if one's opponent has the burden of proof, to dispose of his arguments seems a sufficient defence of one's own position.) And the typical realist argument against idealism is that it makes the success of science a *miracle*. Berkeley needed God just to account for the success of beliefs about tables and chairs (and trees in the Quad); but the appeal to God has gone out of fashion in philosophy, and, in any case, Berkeley's use of God is very odd from the point of view of most theists. And the modern positivist has to leave it without explanation (the realist charges) that 'electron calculi' and 'space-time calculi' and 'DNA calculi' correctly predict observable phenomena if, in

* Lecture II and the first section of Lecture III are an expanded version of 'What is "Realism"?' (© 1976, The Aristotelian Society), a lecture delivered to the Aristotelian Society on 23 February 1976. I am grateful to the Editor of the Aristotelian Society for permission to reprint the paper.

reality, there are no electrons, no curved space-time, and no DNA molecules. If there are such things, then a natural explanation of the success of these theories is that they are *partially true accounts* of how they behave. And a natural account of the way in which scientific theories succeed each other – say, the way in which Einstein's Relativity succeeded Newton's Universal Gravitation – is that a partially correct/partially incorrect account of a theoretical object – say, the gravitational field, or the metric structure of space-time, or both – is replaced by a *better* account of the same object or objects. But if these objects don't really exist at all, then it is a *miracle* that a theory which speaks of gravitational action at a distance successfully predicts phenomena; it is a *miracle* that a theory which speaks of curved space-time successfully predicts phenomena; and the fact that the laws of the former theory are derivable 'in the limit' from the laws of the latter theory has no methodological significance.

I am not claiming that the positivist (or whatever) has no *rejoinder* to make to this sort of argument. He has a number: reductionist theories of the *meaning* of theoretical terms, theories of explanation, etc. Right now, my interest is rather in the following fact: the realist's argument turns on the success of science, or, in an earlier day, the success of commonsense material-object theory. But what does the success of science have to do with the correspondence theory of truth? – or *any* theory of truth, for that matter?

That science succeeds in making many true predictions, devising better ways of controlling nature, etc., is an undoubted empirical fact. If realism is an *explanation* of this fact, realism must itself be an over-arching scientific *hypothesis*. And realists have often embraced this idea, and proclaimed that realism *is* an empirical hypothesis.[1] But then it is left obscure what realism has to do with theory of *truth*. In the present lecture, I shall try to bring out what the connection is between explaining the success of knowledge and the theory of truth.

1 THE 'CONVERGENCE' OF SCIENTIFIC KNOWLEDGE

What I am calling 'realism' is often called 'scientific realism' by its proponents. If I avoid that term here, it is because 'scientific realist', as a label, carries a certain ideological *tone* – a tone more than faintly reminiscent of nineteenth-century materialism, or, to be blunt about it, village atheism. Indeed, if a 'scientific realist' is one who believes, *inter alia*, that *all* knowledge worthy of the name is part of 'science', then I am not a 'scientific realist'. But scientific knowledge is certainly an impressive part of our knowledge, and its nature and significance have concerned all the great philosophers at all interested in epistemology. So it is not surprising that both realists and idealists should claim to be 'philosophers of science', in *two* senses of 'of'. And if I focus on scientific knowledge in what follows, it is because the discussion has focused on it, and not out of a personal commitment to scientism.

To begin with, let me say that I think there *is* something to the idea of *convergence* in scientific knowledge. *What* there is is best explained, in my opinion, in an unpublished essay by Richard Boyd.[2] Boyd points out that all that follows from standard (positivist) philosophy of science is that later theories in a science, if they are to be *better* than the theories they succeed, must imply many of the *observation sentences* of the earlier theories (especially the *true* observation sentences implied by the earlier theories). It does not follow that the later theories must imply the *approximate truth of the theoretical laws of the earlier theories in certain circumstances* – which they typically do. In fact, preserving the *mechanisms* of the earlier theory as often as possible, which is what scientists try to do (or to show that they are 'limiting cases' of new mechanisms), is often the *hardest* way to get a theory which keeps the old observational predictions, where they were correct, and simultaneously incorporates the new observational data. That scientists try to do this – e.g. *preserve* conservation of energy, if they can, rather than postulate violations – is a fact, and that this strategy has led to important discoveries (from the discovery of Neptune to the discovery of the positron) is also a fact.

Boyd tries to spell out realism as an over-arching empirical hypothesis by means of two principles:

(1) Terms in a mature science typically *refer*.
(2) The laws of a theory belonging to a mature science are typically approximately *true*.

Lecture II

What he attempts to show in his essay is that scientists act as they do because they *believe* (1) and (2) and that their strategy works because (1) and (2) are *true*.

One of the most interesting things about this argument is that, if it is correct, the notions of 'truth' and 'reference' have a causal-explanatory role in epistemology. (1) and (2) are premises in an *explanation* of the behaviour of scientists and the success of science – and they essentially contain concepts from referential semantics. Replacing 'true' in premiss (2) (of course, Boyd's argument needs many more premisses than *just* (1) and (2)) by some operationalist 'substitute' – e.g. 'is simple and leads to true predictions' – will not preserve the explanation.

Let us pause to see why. Suppose T_1 is the received theory in some central branch of physics (*physics* surely counts as a 'mature' science if any science does), and I am a scientist trying to find a theory T_2 to replace T_1. (Perhaps I even know of areas in which T_1 leads to false predictions.) If I believe principles (1) and (2), then I know that the laws of T_1 are (probably) approximately true. So T_2 must have a certain property – the property that the laws of T_1 are 'approximately true' *when we judge from the stand-point of* T_2 – or T_2 will (probably) have no chance of being true. Since I want theories that are not *just* 'approximately true', but theories that have a chance of being *true*, I will only consider theories, as candidates for being T_2, which have this property – theories which contain the laws of T_1 as a limiting case. But this is just the feature of the scientific method we discussed. (Boyd also discusses a great many other features of the scientific method – not just this aspect of 'convergence'; but I do not need to go into these other features here.) In fine, my knowledge of the truth of (1) and (2) enables me to restrict the class of candidate-theories I have to consider, and thereby increases my chance of success.

Now, if all I know is that T_1 leads to (mainly) true predictions in some observational vocabulary (a notion I have criticized elsewhere[3]), then all I know about T_2 is that it should imply most of the 'observation sentences' implied by T_1. But it does *not* follow that it must imply the truth of the *laws* of T_1 in some limit. There are many other ways of constructing T_2 so that it will imply the truth of most of the observation sentences of T_1; and making T_2 imply the 'approximate truth' of the *laws* of T_1 is often the *hardest* way. Nor is there any reason why T_2 should have the property that we can assign *referents* to the terms of T_1 from the standpoint of T_2. Yet it is a fact that we can assign a referent to 'gravitational field' in Newtonian theory *from the standpoint of* relativity theory (though not to 'ether' or 'phlogiston'); a referent to Mendel's 'gene' from the standpoint of present-day molecular biology; and a referent to Dalton's 'atom' from the standpoint of quantum mechanics. These retrospective reference assignments depend on a principle that has been called the 'principle of benefit of the doubt' or the 'principle of charity',[4] but not on *unreasonable* 'charity'. Surely the 'gene' discussed in molecular biology is the gene (or rather 'factor') Mendel *intended* to talk about; it is certainly what he should have intended to talk about! Again, if one believes that the terms of T_1 do have referents (and one's semantic theory incorporates the principle of benefit of the doubt), then it will be a *constraint* on T_2, it will narrow the class of candidate-theories, that T_2 must have this property, the property that *from its standpoint* one can assign referents to the terms of T_1. And again, if I do not use the notions of truth and reference in philosophy of science, if all I use are 'global' properties of the order of 'simplicity' and 'leads to true predictions', then I will have no analogue of this constraint, I will not be able to narrow the class of candidate-theories in this way.

2 WHAT IF THERE WERE NO 'CONVERGENCE' IN SCIENTIFIC KNOWLEDGE?

Let me now approach these problems from the other end, from the problem of 'truth'. How would our notions of *truth* and *reference* be affected if we decide *there is no* convergence in knowledge?

This is already the situation according to someone like Kuhn, who is sceptical about convergence and who writes (at least in *The Structure of Scientific Revolutions*) as if the same term cannot have the same referent in different paradigms (theories belonging to or generating different paradigms correspond to different 'worlds', he says), and even more so from Feyerabend's standpoint.

Let us suppose they are right, and that 'electron' in Bohr's theory (the Bohr-Rutherford theory of the early 1900s) does not refer to what we *now* call electrons. Then it doesn't refer to *anything* we recognize in present theory, and, moreover, it doesn't refer to *anything from the standpoint of* present theory (speaking from that standpoint, the only things Bohr *could* have been referring to were electrons, and if he wasn't referring to electrons he wasn't referring to anything). So if we use present theory to answer the question 'was Bohr referring when he used the term "electron"?', the answer has to be 'no', according to Kuhn and Feyerabend. And what other theory can *we* use but our own present theory? (Kant's predicament, one might call this, although Quine is very fond of it too.) Kuhn talks as if each theory does refer – namely, to *its own* 'world' of entities – but that isn't true according to *any* (scientific) theory.

Feyerabend arrives at his position by the following reasoning (which Kuhn does not at all agree with; any similarity in their views on cross-theoretical reference does not come from a shared analysis of science): the introducer of a scientific term, or the experts who use it, accept certain laws as virtually necessary truths about the putative referent. Feyerabend treats these laws, or the theoretical description of the referent based on these laws, as, in effect, a *definition* of the referent (in effect, an *analytic* definition). So if we ever decide that nothing fits that exact *description*, then we must say that there was 'no such thing'. If nothing fits the exact Bohr-Rutherford description of an electron, then 'electron' *in the sense in which Bohr-Rutherford used it* does not refer. Moreover, if the theoretical description of an electron is different in two theories, then the term 'electron' has a different *sense* (since it is synonymous with different descriptions – Feyerabend does not say this explicitly, but if this isn't his argument he doesn't have any) in the two theories. In general, Feyerabend concludes, such a term can have neither a shared referent nor a shared sense in different theories (the 'incommensurability of theories').

This line of reasoning can be blocked by arguing (as I have in various places, and as Saul Kripke has) that scientific terms are not synonymous with descriptions. Moreover, it is an essential principle of semantic methodology that when speakers specify a referent for a term they use by a *description* and, because of mistaken factual beliefs that these speakers have, that description fails to refer, we should assume that they would accept reasonable reformulations of their description (in cases where it is clear, given our knowledge, how their description should be reformulated so as to refer, and there is no ambiguity about how to do it in the practical context). (This is, roughly, the principle of benefit of the doubt alluded to above.)

To give an example: there is nothing in the world which *exactly* fits the Bohr-Rutherford description of an electron. But there are particles which *approximately* fit Bohr's description: they have the right charge, the right mass, and they are responsible for key effects which Bohr-Rutherford explained in terms of 'electrons'; for example, electric current in a wire is flow of these particles. The principle of benefit of the doubt dictates that we treat Bohr as referring to these particles.

Incidentally, if Bohr had not been according the benefit of the doubt to his earlier (Bohr-Rutherford period) self, he would not have *continued to use* the term 'electron' (without even a gloss!) when he participated in the invention of (1930s) quantum mechanics.

Coming back to Kuhn, however: we can answer Kuhn by saying there *are* entities – in fact, just the entities we now call 'electrons' – which behave like Bohr's 'electrons' in many ways (one to each hydrogen atom; negative unit charge; appropriate mass; etc.). And (this is, of course, just answering Kuhn exactly as we answered Feyerabend) the principle of benefit of the doubt dictates that we should, in these circumstances, take Bohr to have been referring to what we call 'electrons'. We should just say we have a different theory of the *same* entities Bohr called 'electrons' back then; his term did refer.

But we can only take this line because present theory does assert the existence of entities which fill many of the *roles* Bohr's 'electrons' were supposed to fill, even if these entities have other, very strange, properties, such as the complementarity of position and momentum, that Bohr-Rutherford 'electrons' were not supposed to have. But what if we accept a theory from the standpoint of which electrons are like *phlogiston*?

Then we will have to say electrons don't really exist. What if this keeps happening? What if *all* the theoretical entities postulated by one generation (molecules, genes, etc., as well as electrons) invariably 'don't exist' from the standpoint of later science? This is, of course, a form of the old sceptical 'argument from

149.94   P983m

error' – how do you know you aren't in error *now*? But it is the form in which the argument from error is a *serious* worry for many people today, and not just a 'philosophical doubt'.

One reason this is a serious worry is that eventually the following meta-induction becomes overwhelmingly compelling: *just as no term used in the science of more than fifty* (or whatever) *years ago referred, so it will turn out that no term used now* (except maybe observation terms, if there are such) *refers*.

It must obviously be a desideratum for the theory of reference that this meta-induction be blocked; that is one justification for the principle of benefit of the doubt. But benefit of the doubt can be *unreasonable*; we don't carry it so far as to say that *phlogiston* referred. If there is no convergence, if later scientific theories cease having earlier theories as 'limiting cases', if Boyd's principles (1) and (2) are clearly false from the point of view of future science, then benefit of the doubt will always turn out to be unreasonable – there will not be a reasonable *modification* of the theoretical descriptions of various entities given by earlier theories which makes those descriptions refer to entities with somewhat the same roles which do exist from the standpoint of the later theory. Reference will collapse.

But what happens to the notion of *truth* in theoretical science if none of the descriptive terms refer? Perhaps all theoretical sentences are 'false'; or some convention for assigning truth-values when predicates don't refer takes over. In any case, the notion of 'truth-value' becomes uninteresting for sentences containing theoretical terms. So truth will collapse too.

Now I want to argue that the foregoing *isn't* quite what would happen. But this will turn on rather subtle logical considerations.

3 MATHEMATICAL INTUITIONISM – AN APPLICATION TO EMPIRICAL KNOWLEDGE

On the assumption that the reader has not studied 'mathematical intuitionism' (the school of mathematical philosophy developed by Brouwer, Heyting, etc.) let me mention a few facts that I will use in what follows.

A key idea of the intuitionists is to use the logical connectives in a 'non-classical' sense. (Of course, intuitionists do this because they regard the 'classical' sense as inapplicable to reasoning about infinite or potentially infinite domains.) They explain this sense – that is, they explain *their* meanings for the logical connectives – in terms of constructive *provability* rather than (classical) truth.

Thus:

(1) Asserting p is asserting *p is provable*. ('p · $\ulcorner p$ is not provable$\urcorner$' is a *contradiction* for the intuitionists.)

(2) '$\neg p$' ($\neg$ is the intuitionist symbol for negation) means *it is provable that a proof of p would imply the provability of $1 = 0$* (or any other patent absurdity). In other words, $\neg p$ asserts the *absurdity of p's provability* (and not the classical 'falsity' of p).

(3) '$p \cdot q$' means *p is provable and q is provable*.

(4) '$p \vee q$' *means there is a proof of p or a proof of q and one can tell which*.

(5) '$p \supset q$' means *there is a method which applied to any proof of p yields a proof of q* (*and a proof that the method does this*).

These meanings are clearly different from the classical ones. For example, $p \vee \neg p$ (which asserts the decidability of every proposition) is not a theorem of intuitionist propositional calculus.

Now, let us *reinterpret* the *classical* connectives as follows:

(1) $\sim$ is identical with $\neg$.

(2) · (classical) is identified with · (intuitionist).

(3) $p \vee q$ (classical) is identified with $\neg(\neg p \cdot \neg q)$.

(4) $p \supset q$ (classical) is identified with $\neg(p \cdot \neg q)$.

Then, with this interpretation, the theorems of *classical* propositional calculus become theorems of intuitionist propositional calculus![5] In other words, this is a *translation* of classical propositional calculus *into* intuitionist propositional calculus – not, of course, in the sense of giving the classical *meanings* of the connectives in terms of intuitionist notions, but in the sense of giving the classical theorems. (It is not the only such 'translation', by the way.) The meanings are still not classical, if the classical connectives are reinterpreted in this way, because these meanings are explained in terms of *provability* and not *truth and falsity*.

To illustrate: classically $p \vee \sim p$ asserts that every proposition is true or is false. Under the above 'conjunction-negation translation' into intuitionist logic, $p \vee \sim p$ asserts $\neg(\neg p \cdot \neg\neg p)$, which says that it is absurd that a proposition and its negation are both absurd – nothing about being true or false!

One can extend all this to the quantifiers – I omit details.

One thing this shows is that contrary to what a number of philosophers – including recently Hacking – have asserted, such inference rules as $p \cdot q / \therefore p;\ p \cdot q / \therefore q;\ p / \therefore p \vee q;\ q / \therefore p \vee q;\ \sim p,\ \sim q / \therefore \ \sim (p \vee q)$ do not fix the 'meanings' of the logical connectives. Someone could accept all of these rules (and all classical tautologies, as well) and still be using the logical connectives in the non-classical sense just described – a sense which is not truth-functional.

Suppose, now, we apply *this* interpretation of the logical connectives (the interpretation given by the 'conjunction-negation translation' above) to empirical science (this idea was suggested to me by reading Dummett on Truth, although he should not be held responsible for it) in the following way: replace *constructive provability* (in the sense of intuitionist mathematics) by *constructive provability from* (some suitable consistent reconstruction of) *the postulates of the empirical science accepted at the time*[6] (or, if one wishes to be a realist about 'observation statements', those together with the set of true observation statements). If the empirical science accepted at the time is itself *inconsistent* with the set of true observation statements – because it implies a false prediction – then some appropriate subset would have to be specified, but I shall not consider here how this might be done. If B_1 is the empirical science accepted at *one* time and B_2 is the empirical science accepted at a *different* time, then, according to this 'quasi-intuitionist' interpretation, the very *logical connectives* would refer to 'provability in B_1' when used in B_1 and to 'provability in B_2' when used in B_2. The *logical connectives* would change meaning in a systematic way as empirical knowledge changed.

4 TRUTH

Suppose we formalize empirical science or some part of empirical science – that is, we formulate it in a formalized language L, with suitable logical rules and axioms, and with empirical postulates appropriate to the body of the theory we are formalizing. Following standard present-day logical practice, the predicate 'true' (as applied to sentences of L) would not itself be a predicate of L, but would belong to a stronger 'meta-language', ML. (Saul Kripke is currently exploring a method of avoiding this separation of object language and meta-language, but this would not affect the present discussion.) This predicate might be defined (using the logical resources of ML but no descriptive vocabulary except that of L) by methods due to Tarski; or it might be taken as a primitive (undefined) notion of ML. In either case, we would wish all sentences of the famous form:

(T) 'Snow is white' is true if and only if snow is white

– all sentences asserting the equivalence of a sentence of L (pretend 'Snow is white' is a sentence of L) and the sentence of ML which says of that sentence that it is true – to be theorems of ML. (Tarski called this 'Criterium W' in his *Wahrheitsbegriff* – and this somehow got translated into English as *'Convention T'*. I shall refer to the requirement that all sentences of the form (T) be theorems of ML as *Criterion T*.)

What happens to 'true' if we reinterpret the logical connectives in the 'quasi-intuitionist' manner just described? *It is possible to define it exactly à la Tarski*. Only 'truth' becomes *provability* (or, to be more precise, the double negation of provability. I shall ignore this last subtlety). In short: the *formal* property of truth– the Criterion of Adequacy (Criterion T) – only *fixes* the extension of 'true' *if the logical connectives are classical*.

This means that we can extend the remark we made in section 3 (the first indented remark): even if the 'natives' we are studying accept the Criterion T in addition to accepting all classical tautologies, it doesn't follow just from that that their 'true' is the classical 'true'.

'Truth' (defined in the standard recursive way, following Tarski) becomes *provability* if the logical connectives are suitably reinterpreted. What does 'reference' become?

On the Tarski definition of truth and reference,

(a) 'Electron' refers

is equivalent to

(b) There are electrons.

But if 'there are' is interpreted intuitionalistically (b) asserts only

(c) There is a description D such that 'D is an electron' is provable in B_1.

And *this* could be true (for suitable B_1) even if there are no electrons! In short, the effect of reinterpreting the logical connectives intuitionalistically is that 'existence' becomes *intra-theoretic*. Actually, the effect is even more complicated than (c) if, in addition to understanding the connectives 'quasi-intuitionalistically' (i.e. in the intuitionist manner, but with 'provability' relativized to B_1), we use the conjunction-negation translation to interpret the 'classical' connectives, as suggested here. But this complication does not change the point just made: if the quantifiers, like the other logical connectives, are interpreted in terms of the notion of *provability*, then existence becomes intra-theoretic.

5 CORRESPONDENCE THEORY OF TRUTH

Now, what I want to suggest (the reader has probably been wondering what all this is leading up to!) is that the effect of abandoning realism – that is, abandoning the belief in any describable world of unobservable things, and accepting in its place the belief that all the 'unobservable things' (and, possibly, the observable things as well) spoken of in any generation's scientific theories, including our own, are *mere* theoretical conveniences, destined to be replaced and supplanted by quite different and unrelated theoretical constructions in the future – would *not* be a total scrapping of the predicates *true* and *refers* in their *formal* aspects. We could, as the above discussion indicates, *keep* formal semantics (including 'Tarski-type' truth-definitions); even keep classical logic; and yet *shift* our notion of 'truth' over to something approximating 'warranted assertibility'. And I believe that this shift is what would in fact happen. (Of course, the formal details are only a rational reconstruction, and not the only possible one at that.)

Of course, there isn't any question of *proving* such a claim. It is speculation about human cognitive nature, couched in the form of a prediction about an hypothetical situation. But what makes it plausible is that just such a substitution – a substitution of 'truth within the theory' or 'warranted assertibility' for the realist notion of truth – has *always* accompanied scepticism about the realist notion from Protagoras to Michael Dummett.

If this is right, then what is the answer to our original question: what is the relation between realist explanations of the scientific method, its success, its convergence, and the realist view of truth?

We remarked at the outset that realists claim to believe in something called a correspondence theory of truth. But what is that?

If I am right, it isn't a different *definition* of truth. There is only one way anyone knows how to *define* 'true' and that is Tarski's way. (Actually, as we mentioned earlier, Saul Kripke has a *new* way – but the difference from Tarski is inessential in this context, although it is important for the treatment of the antinomies.) But is Tarski's way 'realist'?

Well, it depends. If the logical connectives are understood realistically ('classically', as people say), then a Tarski-type truth-definition is 'realist' to at least this degree: satisfaction (of which truth is a special case) is a relation between words and things – more precisely, between formulas and finite sequences of things. ('Satisfies' is the technical term Tarski uses for what I have been calling *reference*. For example, instead of saying '"Electron" refers to electrons', he would say 'The sequence of length one consisting of just x satisfies the formula "Electron (y)" if and only if x is an electron'. 'Satisfies' has the technical advantage of applying to n-place formulas. For example, one can say that the sequence *Abraham; Isaac* satisfies the formula 'x is the father of y'; but it is not customary to use 'refers' in connection with dyadic, etc., formulas, e.g. to say that 'father of' refers to *Abraham; Isaac*.) This certainly conforms to an essential part of the idea of a correspondence theory.

Still, one tends to feel dissatisfied with the Tarski theory as a reconstruction of the 'correspondence theory of truth' *even if* the logical connectives are understood classically. I think that there are a number of sources of this dissatisfaction, which I have expressed myself in some of my writings, but it seems to me that Hartry Field put his finger on the main one: the fact that primitive reference (i.e. *satisfaction* in the case of primitive predicates of the language) is 'explained' by a *list* is the big cause of distress.

But the list has a very special *structure*. Look at the following clauses from the definition of primitive reference:

(1) 'Electron' refers to electrons.
(2) 'Gene' refers to genes.
(3) 'DNA molecule' refers to DNA molecules.

These are similar to the famous

(4) 'Snow is white' is true if and only if snow is white

and the similarity is not coincidental: 'true' is the O-adic case of satisfaction (a formula is true if it has no free variables and the null sequence satisfies it). The Criterion of Adequacy (Criterion T) can be generalized as follows:

(Call the result 'Criterion S' – 'S' for Satisfaction:) An adequate definition of satisfies-in-L must yield as theorems all instances of the following schema: $\ulcorner P(x_1, \ldots, x_n)\urcorner$ is satisfied by the sequence $y_1, \ldots, y_n$ if and only if $P(y_1, \ldots, y_n)$.

Rewriting (1) above as

(1') 'Electron (x)' is satisfied by y_1 if and only if y_1 is an electron
– which is how it would be written in the first place in Tarski-ese – we see that the structure of the list Field objects to is determined by Criterion S. But these criteria – T, or its natural generalization to formulas containing free variables, S – are determined by the formal properties we want the notions of truth and reference to have, by the fact that we *need* for a variety of purposes to have a predicate in our meta-language that satisfies precisely the Criterion S. (This is why we would *keep* Criterion S even if we went over to an Intuitionist or quasi-Intuitionist meaning for the logical connectives.)

So I conclude that Field's objection fails, and that it is correct for the realist to define 'true' *à la* Tarski. Even though the notion of truth is derived, so to speak, by a 'transcendental deduction' (the argument which I gave last time, that we *need* a meta-linguistic notion satisfying Criterion T), and Criterion S is justified similarly, satisfaction or reference is still, viewed from within our realist conceptual scheme, a relation between words and things – and one of explanatory value, as Boyd's argument shows.

Now that I have laid out this argument, let me give a shorter and sloppier argument to somewhat the same effect:

'"Electron" refers to electrons' – *how else* should we say what 'electron' refers to from *within* a conceptual system in which 'electron' is a *primitive* term?

As soon as we *analyse electrons* – say 'electrons are particles with such-and-such mass and negative unit charge' – we can say '"electron" refers to particles of such-and-such mass and negative unit charge' – but then *'charge'* (or whatever the primitive notions may be in our new theory) will be explained 'trivially', that is, in accord with Criterion S. Given the Quinian predicament (Kantian predicament?) that there is a real world *but* we can only describe it in terms of our own conceptual system (Well? We should use someone else's conceptual system?) *is it surprising* that *primitive* reference has this character of apparent triviality? I believe that Field would reply along the following lines: (1) None of this shows that truth and reference *must be* defined *à la* Tarski (i.e. defined *à la* Tarski for some preferred language and extended to other languages *via* translation, as we discussed last time); and (2) None of this shows that a 'physicalistic' theory of reference (or at least of primitive reference, in some suitable sense) *cannot* be given. All we have shown is that a physicalistic theory of reference is not *needed*. But it might be (Field would argue) that one is possible, and that it might greatly enhance our understanding of the phenomenon of reference. After all, a physicalistic theory would not be *incompatible* with Tarskian truth/satisfaction-definitions.

Moreover, Field would argue, in accepting Boyd's account of realism, I have given Field himself strong ammunition. It has just been conceded that reference and truth are notions which enter into at least some *causal* explanations. But an important part of the argument against the valence analogy was that truth and reference are not causal explanatory notions. In one sense they are indeed *not* causal explanatory notions; we still need them to do formal logic, for example, and for the other purposes mentioned last time as well, even if Boyd's causal explanations of the success of science are false. But if they enter into causal explanations at all, is it not possible that their causal-explanatory role justifies looking for a physicalistic account of what truth and reference *are* just as the causal-explanatory role of 'valence' justifies looking for a physicalistic account of what valence *is*?

I don't want to discuss these questions today; they will be the topic of my next lecture.

LECTURE III

In the previous lecture we drew a distinction between understanding truth and the logical connectives realistically or 'classically' (i.e. in terms of classical truth and falsity) and understanding them quasi-intuitionalistically (i.e. in terms of provability in a theory, say, B_1).

What is it to understand truth and the logical connectives realistically? We have seen what it is not: the fact that one accepts classical logic does not show that one understands truth and the logical connectives realistically. (Nor does the fact that one rejects classical logic show that one understands them idealistically. Elsewhere I have proposed interpreting quantum mechanics via a non-standard logic, but not a logic which is to be understood idealistically any more than classical logic is to be understood idealistically.[1]) Nor is it just a question of accepting Criterion T or even Criterion S, or a question of accepting a Tarski-style truth-definition for one's language.

What does show that one understands the notion of truth realistically is one's acceptance of such statements as:

(A) Venus might not have carbon dioxide in
its atmosphere even though it follows
from our theory that Venus has carbon
dioxide in its atmosphere.

and

(B) A statement can be false even though it

34

follows from our theory (or from our
theory plus the set of true observation
sentences).

Now (B) follows from any sentence of the general form (A).
So why do we believe (A) (and many similar sentences)?

Well, even if it were a scientific law (as it of course is not)
that Venus has carbon dioxide in its atmosphere, still 'Venus
has carbon dioxide in its atmosphere' should not be *entailed* by
'it follows from theory B_1 that Venus has carbon dioxide in its
atmosphere' (where B_1 is a formalization of present knowledge).

Of course, 'It follows from theory B_1 that Venus has carbon
dioxide in its atmosphere' and B_1 *together* entail 'Venus has
carbon dioxide in its atmosphere'; but the difficulty is that if
asserting p is reconstrued as asserting 'p is provable in B_1' (or
B_1 plus the set of all true observation sentences) – *if there is no
difference* between the 'speech act' of asserting p and the 'speech
act' of asserting 'p follows from B_1 (plus the set of true observation sentences)' – then for every p, p is *entailed* by 'p follows from
B_1 (plus the set of true observation sentences)'. And then, since
anything that follows from B_1 *alone* certainly follows from the
conjunction of B_1 with the set of true observation sentences,
'p follows from B_1' *entails* p, for any p – which is obviously
nonsense, given normal realistic preconceptions.

That we ordinarily *reject* the equivalence of p and 'p follows
from B_1 (plus the set of true observation sentences)' shows that
our present concept of truth is one in which it is *at least logically*
possible for a statement to follow from B_1 (our best body of
current theory) and not be *true*. But, in fact, we think it is much
more than just *logically* possible that Venus does not have carbon
dioxide in its atmosphere – even if we accept B_1, we think there
is a possibility B_1 might be wrong in a stronger sense than
'logical possibility' – a 'non-zero probability' B_1 might be wrong
– and *this* estimate is *itself* based on our factual beliefs about the
world and how we gather knowledge of it. In short, we view
knowledge itself as the product of certain types of causal interactions, at least in such cases as 'Venus has carbon dioxide in its
atmosphere'. And it *follows from our theory* of the interaction
whereby we learned this fact – for example, the standard causal
account of perception and the theory of error – that we might

have, for any number of reasons, made up a theory from which it follows that Venus has carbon dioxide in its atmosphere, even if it did not. In short, (A) is itself a 'scientific' (or even a *common-sense*) *fact about the world* (albeit a *modal* fact about the world). But given the obviousness and centrality to our understanding of knowledge of facts like (A), how could anyone *not* understand truth and logical connectives realistically? How could anyone not be a realist?

Historically, one possible tack was to *accept* (A), *accept* the 'realist' (classical) logical connectives, but to give an idealist account of the meanings of the descriptive terms (i.e. the predicates, or at least the 'theoretical vocabulary'). But with the failure of the reduction programmes of phenomenalism and logical empiricism, that way was blocked.

Some empiricist philosophers – Peirce, and more recently Sellars – have tried to preserve the idea that B_1 might be false – indeed, that it *will* undoubtedly turn out to be false – without employing a realist notion of truth and falsity, by identifying truth not with *present* 'warranted assertibility' (provability in B_1, or B_1 plus the set of true observation sentences, in our reconstruction) but with warranted assertibility *in the ideal limit* of scientific investigation. Thus B_1 might imply 'Venus has carbon dioxide in its atmosphere', but in the ideal limit of scientific investigation we might eventually accept a theory which says the opposite; and *this* is what Peirce and Sellars take the assertion that Venus might not have carbon dioxide in its atmosphere to *mean*. But this assumes that we can make sense of the notion of an *ideal limit* of scientific investigation without a framework of space-time locations, objects, etc., to specify the manner in which and the conditions under which scientific investigation is to proceed to the limit, which is not the case. Moreover, this assumes convergence. If there is no convergence in general (i.e. if the cases of failure of convergence are more numerous and significant than the cases of convergence) as Kuhn and Feyerabend think, then this 'ideal limit' theory of truth is as badly off as realism is.

The more feasible tack, if one believes that scientific knowledge does not converge, would be to argue that the *phenomenon of scientific revolutions* shows that the realist notion of reference (and hence of truth) leads to disaster (*via* the meta-induction I discussed in the previous lecture) and so we must fall back on an intuitionist or quasi-intuitionist reading of the logical connectives, which would save the bulk of extensional scientific theory, and save the formal part of our theories of reference and truth, at the cost of giving up (A) and (B).

The realist, in effect, argues that science should be taken at 'face value' – without philosophical reinterpretation – in the light of the failure of all serious programmes of philosophical reinterpretation of science, and that science taken at 'face value' *implies* realism. (Realism is, so to speak, 'science's philosophy of science'.) The opponent replies (assuming *no* convergence) that science itself – viewed *diachronically* – refutes realism. But the failure of convergence is crucial to this sort of anti-realist argument. If we were right in claiming that the mature sciences do 'converge' (in a very sophisticated sense), and that that convergence has great explanatory value for the theory of science, then this sort of 'cultural relativist' anti-realism is bankrupt.

To sum up: realism depends on a way of understanding truth, not just a way of *defining* the word 'true'. The concept of truth is *not* philosophically neutral. The catch is that the meaning of 'true' and of the logical connectives is not fixed by their *formal logic*; these are terms that very much fit Quine's account of meaning: that is, these are terms for which the distinction between total theory and term meaning is *useless*. But 'total theory', I have been arguing, means here just that: *total* theory, not just total *logical* theory, but total theory of knowledge; and this involves our theory of nature and of our interactions with nature. Counting (B) as part of science, and blocking the disastrous meta-induction that concludes 'no theoretical term ever refers' by a theory of science which stresses the 'limiting case' relation between successor theories, is part of an outlook which views the scientific method as *dependent on our highest level empirical generalizations about knowledge itself*, construed as an interaction with the world. Both our reasons for believing in a sophisticated version of convergence, such as Boyd's, and our reasons for accepting (B), have to do with our over-all view of *knowledge as part of the subject of our knowledge*.

Idealists have always maintained that our notion of truth depends on our understanding of our theory and of the activity of 'discovering' it *as a whole*. If I am right, then this is an insight of idealism that realists need to accept – though not in the way idealists meant it, of course.

PHYSICALISM AGAIN

We have now digressed from our original purpose of criticizing the 'physicalistic' approach to the topic of reference, but the digression was worth our while, for we have seen that Leeds's elegant reply to Field requires to be understood with caution. Leeds is right in maintaining that our reasons for needing to have a predicate in the language with the *disquotation property* – the property that to ascribe that predicate to any sentence (in a suitable language) is equivalent to asserting that sentence – are not causal-explanatory, and that the formal theory of truth is independent of causal-explanatory considerations. But the notion of truth can be used in causal explanations – the success of a man's behaviour may, after all, depend on the fact that certain of his beliefs are *true* – and the formal logic of 'true' is not all there is to the notion of *truth*.

In order to examine this issue more deeply, let me set up a model. I want to imagine a speaker whose structure is, in a sense, 'transparent' to us. The speaker can be, for the purposes of this science fiction story, an automaton that computes degrees of confirmation (the fact that I don't think this is really a very good way to do inductive logic is irrelevant here), computes utilities in accordance with some built-in utility function, and acts so as to maximize estimated utility. I will assume our 'speaker' (call him 'Karl') speaks an 'unnatural' language – a first-order functional calculus, in fact – and that we are given the translations of the logical words (begging all kinds of questions), but not of any extra-logical (descriptive) vocabulary.

Our problem is to assign a 'meaning', or at least a *reference*, to the extra-logical vocabulary by justifying the selection of a translation or of a truth-definition in the Tarski sense.

Let me now make the following assumption: that the speaker is *reliable*, in the sense that the sentences he utters have a high probability of being true. (This is the case in which the notions of truth and reference are most likely to have causal-explanatory uses.) I am going to look for a translation, or rather a truth-definition, for his language which make this the case. One can view the requirement that the sentences of the corpus have a high probability of being true as a global 'constraint' on translation: this is what has been called the 'principle of charity'. (In this form the principle is wrong, as I have argued elsewhere, but I will stick to this incorrect form as a deliberate over-simplification.)

Now, if there were a *unique* truth-definition which made the speaker *maximally* reliable (i.e. if for any other, non-equivalent truth definition, the speaker's probability of uttering a 'true' sentence in the sense of that truth-definition were lower than the probability of his uttering a sentence which is 'true' in the sense provided by the one in question), and if it were always reasonable to pick the truth-definition which makes the speaker maximally reliable, then *reference* would have the following definition:

To state the definition, we recall that a truth-definition such as the one given in Lecture I defines a relation of *reference* between predicates of the language and suitable objects. Moreover, the relation of reference totally determines the extension of 'true' as applied to that language. Assume (what is actually not the case) that *one unique relation R* is such that if we take R as the relation of reference in a truth-definition for Karl's language then the probability that sentences Karl utters are true – true in the sense of 'true' determined by the choice of R as the relation of reference – is greater than it would have been if we had chosen any other relation R as the relation of reference for Karl's language. In other words, assume that interpreting Karl's utterances in accordance with the truth-definition based on R is *maximally charitable to Karl*. Then define: Karl *refers* to something when he uses a word if and only if he bears that relation R – the one which leads to a truth-definition that is maximally charitable to him – to that something.

As we shall see, this is much too simple. But let us pause for a moment and see what would be the case if it *worked*:

(a) To estimate the *reliability* of Karl, we have to use
   not only a knowledge of Karl's *inductive program*, but
   also of the nature of the *environment*. This is not
   something I find implausible; I have argued
   elsewhere that meaning is a function of the environment

and not just of what is in the heads of speakers.[2]

(b) What Karl refers to depends on the global structure of his 'linguistic' (and inductive) behaviour. Moreover, this will be a feature of *any* theory of reference that incorporates anything *like* a principle of charity.

(c) 'X refers to Y by word Z' is *not* a *physical* relation, if the above definition is correct; it is a *functional* relation, in the sense of using no predicate which refers to the physical-chemical composition of the speaker or the environment.

Even though the above definition cannot be correct, for many reasons, (b) indicates that reference cannot, for example, be defined by 'X refers to Y if and only if X (a particular utterance of X) is connected to Y by a causal chain of the appropriate type'. (Of course, phrases like 'causal chain *of the appropriate* type' are extremely vague, so maybe the causal theories can evade this by allowing global constraints to enter in determining what the 'appropriate type' of causal chain is.)

However, the above definition doesn't work. For as Quine has pointed out, if one truth-definition makes a speaker's utterances true (or some subset of them), so will infinitely many others. Moreover, even if we could somehow fix what the truth-conditions should be for the speaker's sentences *as wholes*, Quine's famous 'gavagai' example, which we shall describe below, indicates that one can find non-coextensive satisfaction definitions which lead to *equivalent* truth-conditions for all *sentences* of L. So 'maximize the reliability ascribed to Karl' – even if it were a correct maxim – would *under-determine* the truth-conditions of Karl's sentences as wholes; and under-determine the *reference* of sentence-*parts*.

So what do we in fact do? I think that in actual translation we start out with assumptions as to what the speaker *wants* or *intends*, at least in many situations. After hours without food, we assume he wants food; after hours awake, he may want to sleep (especially if he is rubbing his eyes); etc. We also assume that his 'reliability' in the abstract sense of truth-probability is not unconnected with his functional *efficiency*. If a speaker accepts a sentence S whenever he is looking at *water*, and he reaches for the water in question whenever he is deprived of water and accepts S, then S might mean 'there's water' or 'there's something to drink', etc.; but it is *unlikely* (to put it mildly) that S means '3 is a prime number'.

This suggests that what we do in 'translation' is to construct a global theory which gives reasonable explanations of the speaker's behaviour in the light of his beliefs (as determined by the translation-manual which is *one* component of the global theory) *and* his desires and intentions (as determined by the psychological theory which is the *other* component).

To avoid one possible misunderstanding, let me say this: I am not just contending that it is *good methodology* in *finding out* what a speaker 'means' to try to *rationalize* his behaviour in this way! I am suggesting that what it is to be a correct translation or truth-definition is to be the translation or truth-definition that best explains the behaviour of the speaker. This is a substantive metaphysical theory of what 'correctness' *is* in linguistics; to challenge it, if they are challenging it, 'physicalists' must produce an alternative theory and show why it is superior.

Now, rationalizing the behaviour of a speaker is *explaining*: e.g. I am willing to *sit* on an object if and only if I accept the sentence 'I won't get hurt, embarrassed, etc., if I sit on this'; and assigning to my utterance the standard truth-conditions (and assuming I generally believe sentences I would assent to, and that goal, belief, and action are linked in the standard way) are all part of *explaining* the fact that I am willing to sit on object Y if and only if I accept the sentence in question. Explaining a large number of facts about a speaker's behaviour-dispositions in just this way is all I mean by the big pretentious expression 'rationalize behaviour'. But *explanation is an interest-relative notion*.

What I want to do next, is explain what I mean by this, and show how what Quine calls the '*indeterminacy of translation*' is, in so far as it exists, *explained by the interest-relativity of explanation*.

INTERESTS AND EXPLANATION

Let me start by explaining what I mean by the 'interest-relativity' of explanation, and then try applying it to the problem of *translation*. There are actually several phenomena I have in mind. Let me illustrate them by a series of examples:

(1) Professor X is found stark naked in the girls' dormitory
at 12 midnight. Explanation: (?) He was stark naked
in the girls' dormitory at midnight $-\epsilon$, and he could
neither leave the dormitory nor put on his clothes
by midnight without exceeding the speed of light. But
(covering law:) nothing (no professor, anyhow) can
travel faster than light.

(2) A peg (1 inch square) goes through a 1 inch square hole
and not through a 1 inch round hole. Explanation: (?)
the peg consists of such-and-such elementary particles
in such-and-such a lattice arrangement. By computing all
the trajectories we can get applying forces to the peg
(subject to the constraint that the forces must not be
so great as to distort the peg or the holes) in the
fashion of the famous Laplacian super-mind, we
determine that some trajectory takes the peg
through the square hole, and no trajectories take
it through the round hole. (covering laws: the
laws of physics.)

(3) Willie Sutton (the famous bank robber) is supposed to
have been asked 'Why do you rob banks?' His reply was
'That's where the money is'. Now (this example is due
to Alan Garfinkel) imagine:
(a) a priest asked the question;
(b) a robber asked the question.

As a preliminary, I should say that I view philosophy of
science as *normative* description of science. From this perspective,
it is clear that explanation has to be partly a *pragmatic* concept.
To regard the 'pragmatics' of explanation as no part of the
concept is to abdicate the job of figuring out *what makes explanations good*. More precisely: the issue is not whether we count the
pragmatic features as 'part of the meaning' – that is a silly kind
of issue in the case of such notions as 'explanation' – but whether
our theory does justice to them or relegates them to mere
'psychology'.

Now (1) and (2) satisfy the standard 'deductive-nomological'
model of explanation. But they are terrible. (Whether one
denies that they are explanations at all – which would be my
sense of both how the language works and how it should work

– or only says that they are *bad* explanations is less important.) Why are they terrible?

(1) is terrible because the whole deduction is from premises we knew to be true when we asked the 'why' question *and* we knew *this* deduction could be given. More deeply: explanations frequently (not always) spring from a desire to know how to bring about or avoid the explanandum, and to do so by means in a specified range. If we ask why professor X was in this shocking condition, we might want to know what sort of motives, or intentions, or neuroses, or anyway *psychological* causes brought about this state of affairs. Even *if* we are *not* interested in prevention or control, usually we want the sort of information we would need *if* we *were* interested in prevention or control. Knowing that we can prevent X's being naked in the dormitory at 12 by preventing him from being naked in the dormitory at $12 - \epsilon$ just pushes the question back in an uninteresting way. Even from the point of view of pure 'understanding' – subsumption under an interesting theory – the same thing is true. (I suspect our standards of 'interest' in the case of pure understanding are not *totally* divorced from our interests in prediction and control, in fact, but I don't have to argue that – and it doesn't mean I think we don't value understanding for its own sake, as of course we do.) So 'why questions' – and hence explanations – *presuppose ranges of interests*.

(2) is terrible for a different reason. It isn't that we *know* or could supply the Laplacian super-mind's deduction. Indeed, if *no* other explanation could in principle be given, maybe this would be 'the' explanation. But in fact there is an explanation – one using only the geometrical fact that a 1-inch square does not fit into a 1-inch circle, and the given fact(s) that the peg and the holes do not change shape (and solid does not pass through solid) which is simpler *and* generalizes to an interesting class of cases. So, (2) violates *methodological* interests, whereas (1) violates *background* interests.

(3) is interesting in another way. The philosopher who invented this case – Alan Garfinkel – speaks of 'Explanatory Relativity'[3] – the idea is that a why-question always presupposes a 'space' of *relevant alternatives*. The priest's question means: 'Why do you rob banks – *as opposed to not robbing at all*?' The robber's question means: 'Why do you rob banks – as opposed to, say, gas

stations?' and Sutton's answer is an answer (or partial answer) to the robber's question, but not the priest's. (One might apply the notion of an 'explanation space' also to (1).)

Now let me shift to Quine's problem of 'radical translation'. I want to modify Quine's famous 'gavagai' example from Ch. II of *Word and Object*. In my version, we have a 'jungle language' with a word 'gavagai' that we would naturally translate as 'rabbit'. Indeed, I will suppose we have a successful smooth-running translation-manual (M) for the jungle language in which 'gavagai' *is* translated as 'rabbit'. The idea is that we *could* construct an alternative translation-manual (M') in which 'gavagai' is translated as 'undetached rabbit-part' (or 'rabbit-stage' or whatever). Moreover, I will suppose M' leads to truth-conditions for *whole sentences* which are easily seen to be equivalent to the ones provided by M – this is a matter of making compensatory adjustments in the translations of *other* words and/or 'taxemes' (features of *arrangement*, such as word-order). (Quine does not speak of preserving truth-conditions but of preserving what he calls 'stimulus meanings'.) Now, Quine's question comes to this: Who's to say (and on what basis) that M is *right* and M' is *wrong*? – that 'gavagai' means *rabbit* and not *undetached rabbit-part*?

Let us apply the idea that *translating* is *rationalizing behaviour*. Consider this case: the native, Karl, sees something and says *gavagai*. He shoots it, and takes it home and cooks it. Why do *we* find it so much more natural to translate 'gavagai' as *rabbit* than as *undetached rabbit-part*?

(1) *Not* because it makes the whole translation manual M 'simpler'. That may be a strong factor *at the end* (when we have constructed M). But I submit we would find *rabbit* the more natural translation even if *gavagai* were the *first* bit of jungle language we had encountered. (Also, the *reason* M is simpler is in large part that *our* language has short expressions for 'rabbit' and not for 'undetached rabbit-part', 'detached rabbit-part', etc.)

(2) The fact is that we find the simplest *explanation* of Karl's behaviour to be something like this: 'He believes he sees a rabbit. He wants a rabbit to eat. So he shoots it.' And 'He believes he sees an undetached rabbit-part. He wishes some undetached rabbit-parts so he can detach them and eat them. So he shoots at one of the undetached rabbit-parts he sees' seems absurd to us, *given the way we structure the explanation-space*, given

what *we* consider the relevant classes of cases to generalize to, etc.

I think that the reason Quine's doctrine of the 'indeterminacy of translation' – extending in this case to an *indeterminacy of reference* (and hence of satisfaction-definitions) – seems so implausible is that we think of the doctrine from the point of view of *our* interests, explanation-spaces, etc. Given all of this, it is indeed unclear that there is any 'indeterminacy'. There may well be a (more-or-less) unique 'correct' translation *for us*. But let us look at the question *not* from the point of view of *one* culture translating the jungle language (and having to choose between M and M') but from the point of view of two cultures *with different interests* translating the *same* jungle language. Suppose the other culture – say Martian – has short expressions for 'undetached rabbit-part' and 'detached rabbit-part' (assuming *our* translation manual for Martian, of course) and parts are of great *interest* to Martians (perhaps they are very *small*, and rabbit-parts, tree-parts, etc., are much more perspicuous for Martians than whole trees and rabbits, of which they have little conception) but there is no short expression for whole rabbits, and whole rabbits, cats, dogs, etc., are not of much interest to Martians in everyday life. Then the Martians might well find the most 'natural' translation of 'gavagai' to be the Martian expression that *we* translate as 'undetached rabbit-part'.[4] In short, 'indeterminacy of translation' (and reference) is plausible to *the extent* that it follows from the interest-relativity of explanation.

LECTURE IV

In the previous lectures I have argued that the formal logic of *true* and *refers* is captured by Tarskian semantics, but the concepts of truth and reference are *undetermined* by their formal logic. The notions of truth and reference can indeed be thought of as defined à la Tarski (for one's own language); but it is only by examining our theory of the world, and specifically by examining the connections between truth and various kinds of provability or warranted assertibility as they are drawn *within* that theory itself, that one can determine whether the notions of truth and reference we employ are realist or idealist, 'classical' or 'intuitionist'.

A second dimension of under-determination appears, as we saw in the last lecture, when we extend the notions of truth and reference to *other* languages – that is, when we speak of what is said in another language as true or as referring to something. Such talk presupposes not only a concept of truth for our own language, but also a mapping of the other language onto our own; and such mappings, I argued in the last lecture, can be relative to our interests. The 'softness' of social facts may affect the 'hard' notions of truth and reference. In the present lecture I want to examine some possible objections to this contention.

One might object to my argument that

interest-relativity of explanation →
(possible) indeterminacy of reference

by contending that the *speaker's* interests are the ones that matter. *Given* these (i.e. assuming a *psychological* description of the speaker *exists*, whether we can in practice *verify* it or not), why should not the reference and meaning of the speaker's words be determinate?

There are *two* assumptions underlying this objection that I reject.

(1) It is assumed (for example, by Peter Winch in his book *The Idea Of A Social Science*) that the speakers' explanation of their own behaviour is necessarily the applicable one. I agree that it always *counts* (in ways it is certainly hard to describe – and impossible to reduce to an algorithm), but it isn't always *right*.

To see that it isn't, let me point out that the interest-relativity of explanation has to be restricted somewhat. My basic standpoint, remember, is that philosophy is (in part) *normative* description of our institutions; theory of knowledge seeks to explain and describe our practice that contributes to the success of inquiry. Now, it contributes to the *usefulness* of the concept of explanation that we reject explanations that don't fit the explanation-space, explanations that generalize to an 'uninteresting' class of cases (like the peg-board example – the Laplacian explanation *versus* the geometrical one), and explanations that simply give back what we already know (the professor in the women's dorm. example). That is why I count such 'pragmatic' features of explanation as the ones illustrated as of *methodological* interest and not *merely* 'psychological' interest. But it does not follow that *any* explanation at all (even one that is 'complete' in the sense of Hempel's model) *can* be *good given suitable interests*. For, given our *normative* outlook, we are only interested in explanations which are compatible with such aims of inquiry as *stating truths, uncovering errors, stating laws* (in the case of scientific inquiry), *finding out what can possibly happen and what is impossible, describing various important kinds of processes, aiding technology and control of nature in general*, etc. Being interested in why Sutton robs banks rather than gas stations and being interested in why he robs banks rather than not robbing at all are *both* compatible with these objectives. That is why this is a genuine case of interest-relativity.

Coming to the 'Martians', even if they explain Karl's behaviour with the rabbit in terms of 'undetached rabbit-parts' rather than rabbits, and even if it is 'natural' for the Martians to do this given *their* interests, conceptual scheme, etc., still, to make this an *interesting* case we have to suppose that the Martians' interests are not arbitrary (given, say, their small size); and that, moreover, the Martians' interests are compatible with developing a science that contains as good a set of 'laws' as ours, is at least as approximately true as ours, is technologically effective, and so on. It is because there is no reason to think that this could not be the case – because a 'rabbit-parts' culture *might* do all this – that this example is of interest. Notice, by the way, that the Martians *can* refer to rabbits when they want to – as 'maximal connected wholes consisting of undetached rabbit-parts', and they may perfectly well realize that rabbits are more *important* than undetached rabbit-parts in *certain contexts* – e.g. the context of biological theory. All I am supposing is that in *daily life* they find it more natural to think and talk of 'seeing undetached rabbit-parts', etc., than of 'seeing rabbits', etc.

Now, it is quite true that when we *or* the Martians explain Karl's behaviour in our respective ways we have to consider not only what he does in the immediate context (he says *gavagai*; he kills the rabbit; he cooks and eats it), but also his total behaviour – *as we 'rationalize' it* (by *translation*) – in particular, Karl's description of his own *intentions*, *interests*, and *desires*. But that does *not* mean that our final explanation of Karl's total behaviour has to be one Karl would accept, given his interests, etc.[1]

For the sake of an example, suppose Karl belongs to a culture which is saturated with the sense-datum theory. Karl may say that the best explanation of why he says *gavagai* is that 'he directly perceives rabbitish sense-data'. And he may reject explanations which include 'he sees a rabbit' as 'metaphysical'. But this doesn't mean that *we* necessarily have to agree *either* that this is a good explanation of Karl's verbal behaviour, *or* that *gavagai* means 'lo, a rabbitish sense-datum' – even if Karl *says* that's what it means. Explicit meta-linguistic statements can be full of all kinds of false theories.

The point is that 'interest-relativity' once conceded cannot be avoided by taking *Karl's* interpretations as the correct ones, as Winch wishes us to do.

(2) The second assumption underlying this objection is that there is an objectively correct and *non-interest-relative* (non-*our*-interest-relative, that means) description of *Karl's* interests – a true 'psychological description' of Karl – whether we can verify

it or not. I want to reject this. For the sake of definiteness let us pretend that human beings are Turing Machines[2] (which I *certainly* don't believe). And let us grant (temporarily, at least) that there is an 'objectively' correct psychological description of Karl *in the sense of a machine table*. Notice that this is *quite* different from supposing that there is an objectively correct description of Karl *in the sense of a psychological theory*, if by a psychological theory is meant a theory which employs notions like *interest, belief, desire*, etc. This is going to be my main point: indeterminacy of translation is equivalent to indeterminacy of the transition from functional organization (in the sense of machine table, or whatever) *to* psychological description.

The point is that a machine table (or any generalization thereof) does not 'label' states or configurations *psychologically*. Even given the machine table, one still has to figure out which configuration corresponds to *believing that P* etc. The fact that the Martian does not agree with us about the translation of Karl's utterances means that he probably would not – indeed, *could* not, if he maintains his translation-scheme – agree with us about the 'labelling' of *functional* configurations with psychological labels. We both agree, let us suppose, that Karl's machine configuration when he says *gavagai* is C. But the Martian says that the proper psychological 'label' for configuration C is 'believing that an undetached rabbit-part is ostended' and *we* say the proper psychological label is 'believing a *rabbit* is ostended'. Whatever makes one label more natural for the Martian than the other makes one translation of *gavagai* more natural, and vice versa. So being a 'realist' with respect to Karl's psychology *in the sense of his functional organization* doesn't help!

But why should we stop short at being realists with respect to functional organization? Why not just be realists with respect to intentions, desires, beliefs – in short, with respect to psychological description in the ordinary sense?

In part, the answer is that this makes it too easy to answer Quine. What a speaker means when he utters U could/can be determined by seeing what *belief* standardly accompanies U (or, perhaps, what belief one standardly *intends* to convey in uttering U, *à la* Grice[3] and Schiffer[4]). This looks like what Quine calls the 'museum myth' of meaning in psychological fancy-dress. (The 'museum myth' is the unhelpful theory that there are objects called 'meanings' and what a sentence means is determined by which of these objects it is 'attached' to.) But perhaps the 'museum myth' is *true*. Perhaps Quine just *is* easy to answer. (This is what Noam Chomsky seems to think.)

REALISM AND EQUIVALENT DESCRIPTIONS

Now consider the following information about Karl. Suppose we are given (1) Karl's functional organization (machine table, or whatever); (2) the psychological 'labels' (from *our* perspective, or *our* 'translation-scheme', or whatever) of the various configurations. I will refer to this as a psychological *theory* of Karl. In fact, it is a very *complete* psychological theory. Since many configurations may not have 'psychological' labels – there may be many kinds of 'intervening variables' – it gives much more information about Karl's internal processes (his 'unconscious' processes, in a certain sense) than any set of statements using *only* 'psychological' language in the ordinary sense possibly could. Call this information about Karl, T. Let T′ be like T except that we use the Martian's psychological labels in constructing T′. Then T and T′ will be closely related; in fact, there will be a 'translation-scheme' which carries any description in the language of T into a description in the language of T′ and vice versa. T and T′ have the *same class of models*. They are, by any reasonable standard, *equivalent descriptions* of Karl's psychology – even though one says 'Karl thinks he sees a rabbit', and the other says 'Karl thinks he sees an undetached rabbit-part.'

Now it is easy to see what is wrong with Chomskian 'realism' about psychology: it *ignores the existence of such pairs of equivalent descriptions*.

A twentieth-century realist *cannot* ignore the existence of equivalent descriptions: realism is not committed to there being one true theory (and *only* one). This is as true in psychology as elsewhere. Assuming there is a 'fact of the matter' as to 'which is true' (if either) *whenever* we have two intuitively 'different' theories, is naive. 'Theories' which differ on which pairs of events are *simultaneous* are certainly 'intuitively different', but after Einstein we know such 'theories' may, none the less, be *equivalent*. If the *gavagai* example could be worked out (if there *were* such 'Martians'), it would yield a similar example of 'intuitively different' but *equivalent* 'theories' in *psychology*: that is why saying 'why shouldn't we be just as much realists in psychology as in physics?' is no *answer* to Quine: the counter is, of course, that we *should* be 'realists' in both areas – *sophisticated* realists. And a sophisticated realist recognizes the existence of equivalent descriptions, because it follows from his theory of the world that there are these various descriptions, as it follows from a geographer's description of the earth that there are alternative mappings (mercator, polar, etc.).

DIGRESSION

There is another possible argument which I don't want to go into in any detail (because I'm unsure and because it's too hairy), but which I want to mention. Namely, one could argue that functional organization *itself* is an interest-relative notion. Consider the simplest case, saying that something is a Turing Machine of a certain type (specified by giving a machine table T). Let's say that T is a two-state table. Now, something no one would *consider* to be a machine of type T may actually turn out to *be* a machine of type T under a weird ('artificial') way of specifying what states S_1 and S_2 are. What does this 'weirdness', this 'artificiality' come to? It's not, as one might first suppose, that in a 'kosher' example of a machine of type T the micro-structural predicates P_1, P_2 that 'realize' the *abstractly defined* 'logical states' S_1, S_2 have to be 'natural predicates' from the point of view of physicists. That would rule out such predicates as 'being an inscription of the script letter *a*', which seem perfectly all right. It is rather that the machine table (with P_1, P_2 put in place of the 'logical states' S_1, S_2 that they 'realize') has convincingly to *explain* the machine's behaviour. So the notion of functional organization, it may be argued, also involves a hidden reference to *explanation*, and may, therefore, 'inherit' the interest-relativity of explanation.

The reason I do not regard this argument as being as convincing as the preceding one is this:

If a difference in interests *merely* leads people to regard different predicates as 'natural' (*rabbit versus rabbit-part*), then in general both sets of interests will be compatible with the interests of *science*. This would not be the case if all explanations and descriptions were *part of* theoretical and experimental science, or if the purpose of all explanation were the advancement of theoretical and experimental science. But when we explain someone's behaviour by saying 'he got angry', for example, we do not worry about the fact that 'angry' is a rather broad ordinary language term, and not a term from a psychological theory, or about the fact that an ideal psychological theory would certainly replace the ordinary language notion 'angry' with a battery of more technical concepts, just as physics replaced the ordinary language notion of energy with a battery of technical concepts (some of which kept the old name, e.g. 'kinetic energy'). Although good explanations should not block the progress of scientific inquiry, that does not mean that explanations designed for the purposes of everyday life, or of industry, or even of applied science, must use the categories that would be ideal from the point of view of pure science. The Martians can perfectly well describe the state of affairs that we would describe as 'hunting a rabbit so one can cook it and eat it' as 'hunting undetached rabbit-parts so that one can cook them and detach them and eat them' – indeed, are these not two descriptions of the very same intention? But their use of rabbit-part talk in daily life does not preclude them from having a *technical* term for 'rabbit' which they would use in suitable scientific contexts.

To a certain extent interests can lead one to see processes in the world as exhibiting different causes and yet be equally compatible with science. To use an example essentially due to Hart and Honore:[5] the doctor may see a heart attack as caused by high blood pressure, and the patient's wife may see it as caused by over-indulgence in food and drink, and both may be correct. But this is a case of focusing attention on different parts of one causal mechanism, while difference over machine table is difference over the *global* causal mechanism. That interests could lead one to see processes in the world as exhibiting different global causal mechanisms and yet be equally compatible with the interests of science seems false to me. Thus the interest-relativity (in principle) of functional organization may be quite uninteresting, while the interest-relativity of the step *from* functional organization to *psychology* may be quite interesting. It is because intuitively different psychological theories could agree with the *same* functional organization that they could, for example, link up equally well with molecular biology, etc. (Like all equivalent descriptions, T and T' above exhibit *invariants* – the functional organization.)

Another thing I'm unsure about is this. *If* functional organization did turn out to be significantly interest-relative, would we be *content* with this, or would we want to *remove* the relativity by *restricting* the class of Ps that could be admissible realizations for logical states S? (One reason we might want to do this is that otherwise – if functionalism is right – such predicates as *conscious* would turn out to be interest-relative.)

ANOTHER OBJECTION

This is rather vague, but I often get it, especially from Chomskians. It is usually stated thus: 'In so far as explanation is interest-relative, it is interest-relative in all sciences, physics as much as psychology. So you haven't shown there is any special reason to regard psychology (and translation) as more indeterminate than *physics*.'

This seems to be a bad reply to *Quine*, actually, because Quine is arguing that there is 'under-determination' *for the same reasons* in both physics and psychology, *and* the 'under-determination' in psychology *remains* even if we 'fix' the physics.

My own reply is this: I don't claim that the interest-relativity of explanation *always* implies we can get *equivalent descriptions* in every field and in every vocabulary. Most often it just leads to theories *which answer different questions*. In the *gavagai* example, as I modified it, this is, indeed, what probably happened at first: the Martian wondered why Karl pointed to an undetached goose-part, and not a man-part, etc.; *we* wondered why he pointed to a rabbit and not a goose, tree, man, etc. But if both translation schemes are to be compatible with scientifically acceptable psychology, they must be compatible with psychological theories which are equivalent descriptions, even if they are intuitively 'different'. There is *no* methodological principle, I repeat, which says *these* always exist. Moreover, even when we *have* equivalent descriptions in, say, physics, they are not always in the same vocabulary. A particle/action-at-a-distance theory and a field/contact-action theory may be equivalent descriptions, but they do not employ the same vocabulary.

To show that T_1, T_2 are equivalent descriptions (in the same vocabulary) one commonly shows that they agree on certain 'invariants' *and* argues (in terms of the explanatory role of the invariants) that this is all they *should* agree on: that the invariants give a 'complete' picture of what is going on. In addition, T_1 and T_2 – the 'equivalence' of T_1 and T_2, rather – must not be an instance of what has been called 'trivial semantic conventionality'– just changing the reference of some word in an arbitrary way. It is because Einstein *was* able to argue that (1) *his* invariants *do* give a physically complete description of processes; and (2) that using 'simultaneous' to mean 'simultaneous in Frame 1' is just as O.K. (in agreement with usage, or what have you) as using it to mean 'simultaneous in Frame 2', that the relativity of simultaneity in the Special Theory of Relativity is a *non-trivial* and *correct* example of equivalent descriptions.

What I have tried to do in this lecture, is to suggest a set of *psychological invariants* – the functional organization – such that different translation-schemes might plausibly *agree* with those invariants. This is at least sketching a *specific* way in which translation can be interest-relative: not deducing that it must be from any universal methodological principle. It is because ordinary language psychological explanations are *not* as logically tight as specifications of a functional organization that they could be permuted *within* the bounds set by a specification (up to isomorphism of models) of functional organization. And, since functional organization does constitute an appropriate notion of 'invariant description' for *psychology* (I believe), this means that ordinary language psychological theories and translation schemes can be *different* but equivalent.

LECTURE V

The interest-relativity of explanation may make translation easier at the beginning (if Karl says '*gavagai*', and the relevant cue is always a rabbit, we translate 'gavagai' as *rabbit* without worrying about the possibility of such translations as 'rabbithood again' or 'undetached rabbit-part'); but if what we are doing is *forcing* our pattern of thought on a linguistic scheme which doesn't have *structural* similarities to ours, one which doesn't 'map' onto ours under any mapping that is 'natural' (to us), we would expect to pay a price later, when we try to extend our first translations of isolated utterances to a scheme for interpreting the whole language.

This naturally raises the question: if translation (like all psychological explanation) is interest-relative in principle, why isn't it more difficult than it seems to be?

Part of the answer is that it *is*. As the son of a translator, I know very well that translation isn't easy. And just looking at different translations illustrates some of the interest-relativity that does exist in practice. Still, where common words and unsubtle locutions are involved, translation is pretty determinate. Nobody who knows modern Hebrew doubts that *galgal* means *wheel* and not 'undetached wheel-part', for example. Why is translation as determinate as it is?

To drive the point home, let me point out that 'radical translation' is a *teachable skill*. Kenneth Pike, a Professor of Linguistics at Michigan, has for years *demonstrated on stage* how in an hour or so he can learn enough of a totally *alien* language to get a conversation going. And he *teaches his students* to do the same (some of them to go into the Amazon, where this skill may save their lives).

If translation were as indeterminate in *practice* as it may be in principle, Pike's 'skill' would be unlearnable (in fact, he wouldn't have it), and the *universal intercommunicability of human cultures* would not exist.

There seems only one possible explanation: human *interests*, human *saliencies*, human cognitive processes, must have a *structure* which is heavily determined by innate or constitutional factors. Human nature isn't all *that* plastic.

But if that is so, then the question arises why not take the interests, the saliencies, the 'constraints' that humans innately bring to translation (as opposed to the ones which are mere cultural artifacts) and 'build them in' to the *notion* of translation? Why not overcome the 'interest-relativity' by 'fixing' the interests – this time taking the *invariant*, biologically specified interests, saliencies, priorities, etc.? Of course, they needn't be entirely innate – even if what is innate is a structure which guarantees a *propensity* to certain interests in a very wide range of environments (including all or almost all actual human cultural/physical environments) that would be enough.

I think there are three things wrong with this proposal.

Even if we could determine the 'constraints on radical translation' that we intuitively and preconsciously (if not *un*consciously) employ, 'building these in' to the *notion* of translation would be wrong. For:

(1) If this program succeeded it would yield a ridiculously complicated operationalist analysis (in fact, an 'operational definition') of translation, rather than any theory of the *nature* of translation. But the latter is what a good account of translation should give us. The theory that a translation into our language is a correlation which we use to project our patterns of psychological explanation – the ones we apply to speakers of *our* language – or approximations to those patterns, onto the speakers of the alien language *does* give a theory of the *nature* of translation, even though it doesn't yield 'constraints' in any obvious way.

(2) Like all operationalist analyses, it would be *wrong* (except as an approximation). A definition of 'translation' from which it followed that our hypothetical Martians weren't *translating*

(because their interests and saliencies are different) would be simply wrong.

(3) Such a program (the program of explicating the notion of translation *via* a set of 'constraints' – ignoring for the moment where the constraints come from, innate human nature, our culture, or whatever) is wholly unworkable in *practice*.

Several million dollars and many man-hours of bright people's time was spent on *just* this project – the project of making *explicit* the constraints involved in translation – under the name 'mechanical translation'. Result: essentially, *complete failure*. Chomsky said from the beginning that one couldn't simulate translation without simulating full human capacity, and he was proved right. Now a similar view has been advanced by Marvin Minsky (a leading figure in the Artificial Intelligence Group at MIT) under the name 'theory of frames'. Minsky's idea is that discourse can't be translated without bringing to it a 'frame' of relevant information organized in a suitable way. There is, in Minsky's view, no such thing as a theory of translation *in general* – just a theory for each 'frame'. To simulate translation in general, radical translation, one would have to have a simulation of full human intelligence, saliencies, etc.

What moral follows from all this? The moral I want to draw is something like this: *the notion of translation* (and, if my argument is right, everything I am saying about translation goes for *reference* as well) *cannot be made scientifically precise* (at least not in the foreseeable future; and very likely *never*). *Yet it is perfectly usable in daily life and even in parts of the science of linguistics* (dictionaries are parts of linguistics in any non-purist sense of 'linguistics', for example). (The point that a term which cannot itself be made 'scientifically precise' may be indispensable *even in science* seems to me to be very important, and I shall expand on it in the next lecture.)

Now the program of *defining* reference in terms of 'causal chains' etc. (Field's program, with which I started these lectures) may seem different from the program of *defining* translation by a set of 'constraints'; but the difference is superficial. As soon as one tries to broaden the causal theory so as to cover, say, theoretical terms in science ('electron'), then the principle of the benefit of the doubt comes in, in some version or other – the principle that says that to find out what Bohr referred to by 'electron' in

1904 we must see what would be reasonable reformulations of the descriptions he gave which failed to refer (because, for example, they violated the principle of complementarity that Bohr himself enunciated thirty years later); and giving any *precise* analysis of the notion of a *reasonable* reformulation of a definite description is, if anything, *more* hopeless than giving a precise list of constraints on translation. And the problems are very similar: both reference-assignment and translation depend on choosing 'reasonably' to pair up not-exactly-matching sets of beliefs. To simulate (or even precisely to define) 'reasonableness' is to simulate (or at least define) full human capacity. In short, Field's program is a species of *scientific utopianism*.

To say this is not to repudiate the 'causal theory of reference' (I would rather call it the 'social co-operation plus contribution of the environment theory of the *specification* of reference') that Kripke put forward[1] and that I developed in 'The Meaning of "Meaning"'.[2] Kripke and I were doing two things:

1 We were attacking the idea that speakers pick out referents in the following way: each term T is 'associated' by each speaker with a property P_T (the 'intension' of T). The term applies to whatever has the property P_T.

2 We were giving an alternative account of how speakers *do* pick out referents if they don't associate terms with necessary and sufficient conditions (or properties P_T) as required by, say, Russell's theory.

Both (1) and (2) still seem right to me, and worth doing. But a theory of how reference is *specified* isn't a theory of what reference *is*; in fact, it *presupposes* the notion of reference.

Let me return for a moment to the problem of mechanical translation. Actually, the project of mechanical translation wasn't to 'make explicit the constraints on translation', as I wrote above; it was to make explicit what Quine calls the 'analytical hypothesis' or 'translation manual'. But this is all the better for my argument: 'constraints on translation' are rules for choosing between translation manuals, and it turns out that the 'translation manuals' *exist* only – ONLY! – as embodied human skills!

I want to devote the remainder of this lecture to a closer look at 'scientific utopianism'. This will pave the way for the next (and final) lecture, which will deal with the character of the social sciences (or studies) in general.

Lecture V

AM I SAYING THAT WE CAN'T DO SOMETHING 'IN PRINCIPLE'?

Whenever one uses such an epithet as 'scientific utopianism' one can expect a certain question. Sooner or later – usually sooner rather than later – someone asks whether one is saying that the laws governing human psychology, or whatever, *couldn't* be known 'in principle'; whether one is saying that there is something we can do in physics that it is impossible 'in principle' to do in psychology. I want to argue that in an important sense of 'in principle' – though not a sense the questioner stops to think of in his enthusiasm for 'physicalism' – the answer may well be 'yes'. But even more important in my opinion is the fact that this is very much the wrong question to ask, unless one follows it with *some* discussion of whether what might be done 'in principle' can be done in *practice*.

Obviously there is progress in our understanding of man and society. While few sociologists are 'Marxists' in the sense of holding Marx's work immune from criticism or of sharing Marx's belief in a utopian future, something Marx did teach all students of society is that social forms succeed one another somewhat as species of trees succeed one another in a forest, one providing favourable conditions for the appearance of the next; and that economic organization places important constraints on social organization – even if it is highly controversial what those constraints are and how they operate. And while few psychologists are 'Freudians', something Freud did teach all of us is that our so-called 'conscious lives' emerge out of and float on top of a vast sea of largely unconscious 'selfish fantasy' (to use Iris Murdoch's term). At the other extreme – the more mathematical extreme – of social science, quantitative models have shed light on phenomena ranging from macro-economics to the so-called 'law of effect' in learning theory. But it is important to realize that when one dreams of explicitly defining a notion like 'translation' or 'explanation' or 'reasonable' one is dreaming of something which is quite different from *everything* that has been accomplished so far. As I already remarked, *everything we know* is used in translation (and also in explanation, and in deciding what is 'reasonable'). There is no reason to think one could explicitly define any of these notions in the way physicalist philosophers wish to, or that one could make explicit all the 'constraints' we unconsciously impose on the use of these notions, without having available a *detailed explanatory model of the functional organization of a whole human being*. And this, I contend, it is utopian to expect.

EXPLANATORY MODELS AND NATURAL KINDS

Let me leave our topic for a moment and discuss what it is to have a detailed explanatory model of a natural kind. Our paradigm of such a model is a set of laws together with a description of the features of a member of the natural kind such that our Laplacian super-mind (in conversation, Carnap used to call him 'Logically Omniscient Jones') could 'in principle' deduce the behaviour (or the statistical distribution of behaviours, in the case of an indeterministic theory) of a member of the natural kind from the laws together with (a) the description in question; (b) the values of various parameters in the case of the member in question; (c) the values of various parameters describing 'initial conditions' and 'boundary conditions'.

In addition, the laws and the description should together *explain* the behaviour of the members of the kind; the peg-board example already shows that not every deduction that Logically Omniscient Jones could make counts as an explanation. In particular, this means that, although we do not require that the behaviour of a member of the natural kind could *actually* be predicted in practice by a deduction that it is feasible to carry out, still some range of facts about that behaviour satisfying the usual desiderata in the case of explanation by means of scientific theories – generality, significant variety, significance and fruitfulness – must be deducible from the laws and the description together with suitable auxiliary statements; and that those deductions should satisfy the 'interest' constraints that we described.

What I have described is the explanatory ideal of *physics*, and *in physics* it is sometimes realized to a very high degree of approximation. (An example of such an explanatory model, in the case of the natural kind 'hydrogen atom', would be the laws of quantum mechanics together with the description of the hydrogen atom as consisting of one electron and one proton in a bound state.)

Such a pair, consisting of a set of laws and a description, is not necessarily *enough* however. The following is *not* an example of an explanatory model of the natural kind 'human being'; the laws of physics *plus* the description 'a human being is a physical system consisting of elementary particles'. Why not? After all, if physicalism is true, *this* is a description from which *given the values of the various parameters* (i.e. told *which* elementary particles and in what arrangement, and told the 'initial conditions' and 'boundary conditions') Logically Omniscient Jones *could* deduce the behaviour of an arbitrary member of the kind!

What is wrong is that this is an explanatory model of the wider genus 'physical system' (in a disguised form) and not of the species 'human being'. To ensure that a model of any *genus* (up to and including 'physical system') will not trivially count as an explanatory model of every species, we must require that the following subjunctive conditional be true: *anything that might satisfy the description in question would be a member of the natural kind in question.* Since even the indicative statement that 'every physical system is a human being' is false, let alone the subjunctive conditional that *anything that might be a physical system would be a human being,* the pair consisting of the laws of physics *plus* the statement 'a human being is a system of elementary particles' does *not* count as an explanatory model of a human being.

Moreover, in order to take care of the fact that the laws of quantum mechanics (or of physics as stated at *any* time) are undoubtedly only approximately true, and that, hence, it may *not* be the case that any system consisting of a proton *as we now define 'proton'* and an electron *as we now define 'electron'* would be a hydrogen atom, one has either to specify that the principle of benefit of the doubt is to be used in evaluating the truth of the subjunctive conditional 'anything that might consist of an electron and a proton in a bound state would be a hydrogen atom', or to specify that the truth is to be judged 'from within' the conceptual system to which the theory in question belongs. The point is that the conditional 'everything that might be a system of elementary particles would be a human being' is not true, even if we apply benefit of the doubt to the referring expressions 'system of elementary particles' and 'human being', nor is it true taking present-day science at 'face value', i.e. ignoring the fact that it is only *approximately* true.

When we say that even the explanatory models that physics provides for such natural kinds as 'hydrogen atom' are only approximately correct, we should not lose sight of the fact that for most purposes the degree of approximation can be very high indeed. (In the case of hydrogen atoms, phenomena can be predicted to eight decimal places in quantum electrodynamics.)

What I maintain, again, is that there is a fundamental difference between physics and the social sciences (or better, social *studies*) in this respect. Physics does provide detailed explanatory models of such natural kinds. But we are not, realistically, going to get a detailed explanatory model for the natural kind 'human being'. And the difficulty does not have to do with *mere* complexity. Meteorologists do have a mathematical model of the *weather* (or of many kinds of weather phenomena), although (notoriously) they cannot predict the weather very well in practice because (a) the values of the requisite parameters are not all accurately known; and (b) the computations would be too complex to carry out even if they were known. The reason one can have a fairly simple mathematical model of the natural kind 'weather' is that, although the weather is a mess, it is a relatively unstructured mess. What causes problems for the theorist, as opposed to the engineer, is not complexity *per se*, but highly structured complexity – that is, complexity of structure.

'IN PRINCIPLE' AND 'IN PRACTICE'

Before we discuss what we might or might not be able to do 'in principle', let us discuss what we can reasonably hope to do in practice. Although some people *do* think that it will eventually be possible to construct a detailed explanatory model of a human being, or at least to specify those features of such a model that would constitute the normal-form psychological description of a human being (what I referred to as our 'functional organization' in the previous lecture), no sane student of these matters expects us to achieve this in less than three hundred years. 'But that's a mere empirical fact.' It is an empirical fact, all right, but it isn't so 'mere'.

Philosophers have always claimed to be putting forward 'necessary truths', and they dislike making statements that are clearly 'empirical'. But this may be a very bad trait of philosophers. Some 'empirical' facts may be *constitutive* of our present nature and institutions.

Thus, suppose our functional organization became transparent to us. Suppose we had a theory of it, and we could actually *use* this theory in a significant class of cases. What would happen to us? (If we had the theory but couldn't use it to predict and modify behaviour, it would probably have very little significance for us.) Would it be possible to *love* someone, if we could actually carry out *calculations* of the form: 'If I say X, the probability is 15 per cent she will react in manner Y'? Would it be possible to have friendships or hostilities? Would it be possible even to think of *oneself* as a *person*? I don't know the answer to these questions, but it seems clear that the development of *that* sort of knowledge of ourselves and each other would modify our natures in ways that we cannot predict at all. Every institution we now have: art, politics, religion – even science – would be changed beyond recognition.

But a fact, however 'empirical', which underlies our entire history and which influences the character of every one of our institutions is not 'mere'. The fact that we are partially opaque to ourselves, in the sense of *not* having the ability to understand one another as we understand hydrogen atoms, is such a fact, a *constitutive* fact. If it stops obtaining after, say, three hundred years, well and good; I am not writing philosophy for the next historical epoch and for our post-human descendants; I am writing for human beings in the present period.

WHAT 'IN PRINCIPLE' MEANS AND WHAT IT SHOULD MEAN

Usually philosophers only distinguish two or three notions of possibility: what is possible in the sense of 'logically possible'; what is physically possible in the sense of 'not contrary to any natural laws'; and what is technically possible given our existing technology. 'Is it possible "in principle" to do X?' typically means 'Is X physically possible (or, perhaps, logically possible) to do?' But this is not what 'possible in principle' *should* mean in discussions of such topics as the one we are discussing. There is an important 'in between' notion of possibility (in between physical possibility and technical possibility) that has been left out.

To describe this sense, consider the often-discussed question as to whether human behaviour can be *predicted* 'in principle' (to within the bounds set by quantum-mechanical indeterminacy). The interesting question is not whether Logically Omniscient Jones could do this (i.e. is it logically possible?); nor even whether it is physically possible for a computing system to do this; but rather whether it is physically possible to do this *fast enough to count as a prediction*, whether it is possible to make such a computation 'in real time', as computer people say. And while it may follow from the 'hypothesis of physicalism' that it must be possible for Logically Omniscient Jones to predict our behaviour from an ideal theory (to within the limits set by the indeterminacy of the elementary processes), and it may even follow that it must be physically possible (although I don't believe that it does), there is no reason at all to believe, on that basis or on any other, that it must be possible to do it *in real time*. It may be, for example, that the shortest deduction of what I will do five minutes from now (or of the probabilities of the various alternatives) *would take more than a thousand years to compute* for an optimal computing system using an ideal theory of me and an optimal theorem-proving program. In that case this would be a sense of 'in principle' in which my behaviour wouldn't be predictable *in principle* in this way – even though Logically Omniscient Jones could make the (indeterministic) prediction. Computer science has given us a new concept of 'in principle' with its notion of 'real time computability' – one far more relevant to discussions of predictability than the standard ones.

What goes for prediction also goes for explanation. Human functional organization evolved over one to two million years. There is no reason that it must have a description that would fit into one book, or even into the Bodleian Library. To speak of explaining, not some very general facts about human psychology, but such specific phenomena as why we find some explanations 'natural' and not others, or why we find some views 'unreasonable', or even to deduce any characterization at all of such matters from a hypothetical description of our functional organization may well require so much 'real time' that the human race will have long ceased to exist before such a deduction is carried out!

The problem is that our best current theory of these matters suggests that certain human abilities – language speaking is the paradigm example – may not be theoretically explicable in isolation; it is almost certainly impossible to 'model' a language speaker without modelling full human functional organization. But the latter may well be *unintelligible* to humans when stated in any detail! The moral is not that we can't study ourselves at all; but that (in practice, and, I am arguing, quite possibly 'in prin-ciple') we can't study ourselves the way we study hydrogen atoms.

LECTURE VI

Today I want to discuss some general questions concerning the methods and character of the social sciences. Empiricist philosophers of science, from Mill to the logical empiricists, have tended to take physics as the Platonic idea of a science, and to look forward to the happy day when the social sciences would, by the grace of the 'scientific method', look just like physics. Mill's statement that 'the backward state of the Moral Sciences can only be remedied by applying to them the methods of Physical Science, duly extended and generalized'[1] sets the tone; Zilsel's statements that 'by collecting and comparing the material with philological accuracy historical laws will be discovered at last not by general methodological discussions like ours';[2] and that 'physics is the most mature of all empirical sciences as to method. In physics the law-concept has been used for three hundred years. It is to be assumed, therefore, that most of the difficulties in its application to other fields have their physical counterpart and can be clarified most easily with the help of physical concepts';[3] and Nagel's statement that 'there appears to be no good reason for claiming that the general pattern of explanations in historical inquiry, or the logical structure of the conceptual tools employed in it, differs from those encountered in the generalizing and the natural science'[4] only reaffirm Mill's assertion in various modern accents. The emphasis on physics is revealed by the fact that Nagel, immediately after making the statement just quoted, goes on to say that the 'explanatory premises in history' include laws 'as well as many explicitly (although usually incompletely) formulated singular statements of initial conditions'. 'Law' and 'initial conditions' are physicist's jargon, after all, and not any historian's way of speaking.

As one might expect, the claim, advanced by some of the greatest of the nineteenth-century sociologists, that *Verstehen – the ability to imagine what it would be like to be*, say, a knight in the army of Richard the Lionheart, or a follower of Savonarola – is of methodological as opposed to merely psychological significance in the social sciences is anathema to Nagel *et al.*

According to these empiricist philosophers of science, *Verstehen* (empathetic understanding) may be a source of hypotheses in the social sciences, but not a method of confirmation. Hypotheses must be confirmed by deriving predictions, comparing them with data, etc. In the case of history, hypotheses must include or presuppose *general laws*, which are themselves confirmed by deriving predictions, etc. The two leading ideas are:

(I) The methods of physics (as described by Mill,
     Nagel, etc.) are the methods – the only methods –
     of *all* the sciences.
(II) Knowledge = science = the 'scientific method', i.e.
     anything that can be *known* at all can be known by
     these methods. The hypothetico-deductive method and
     its simpler inductive relatives (plus, of course,
     observation) are all the methods there are for gaining
     non-demonstrative knowledge.

Let me speak to (II) first. (II) is ambiguous: it may mean that, as *a hypothesis in cognitive psychology*, anything we know is learned via a process that fits the paradigms of inductive logic – possibly an unconscious process. (Even one we couldn't write out in full.) Or it may mean that anything we know *could be checked* following the paradigms of inductive logic.

Ernest Nagel wavers curiously on this very question. He writes:

Doubtless the basic trouble in this area of inquiry is that
we do not possess at present a generally accepted, explicitly
formulated, and fully comprehensive schema for weighing
the evidence for any arbitrarily given hypothesis so that
the logical worth of alternate conclusions relative to the
evidence available for each can be compared. Judgments

must be formed even on matters of supreme practical importance on the basis of only vaguely understood considerations; and, in the absence of a standard logical canon for estimating the degree in which the evidence supports a conclusion, when judgments are in conflict each often appears to be the outcome of an essentially arbitrary procedure. This circumstance affects the standing of the historian's conclusions in the same manner as the findings of other students. Fortunately, though the range of possible disagreement concerning the force of evidence for a given statement is theoretically limitless, there is substantial agreement among men experienced in relevant matters on the relative probabilities to be assigned to many hypotheses. Such agreement indicates that, despite the absence of an explicitly formulated logic, many unformulated habits of thought embody factually warrantable principles of inference. Accordingly, although there are often legitimate grounds for doubt concerning the validity of specific causal imputations in history, there appears to be no compelling reason for converting such doubt into wholesale skepticism.[5]

On the one hand, this paragraph can be read as a hypothesis about our 'unformulated habits of thought' (and about we-know-not-what 'factually warrantable principles of inference'). Who would deny that the 'unformulated habits of thought' of a good historian embody *some* 'factually warrantable principles of inference' or other? Perhaps 'rely on *Verstehen* to a certain extent' is a 'factually warrantable principle of inference'! On the other hand, the qualifiers 'at present' and 'explicitly formulated' (in the statement that 'we do not possess at present a generally accepted, *explicitly formulated*, and fully comprehensive schema for weighing the evidence') suggests that all science – including history, which is the topic of Nagel's paper – *might* be done by following a 'standard logical canon' which itself represents an elaboration of the standard account of the methodology of 'the generalizing and the natural sciences' – that is, of *physics*. I will assume this latter interpretation of Nagel's words, since only on this interpretation was he talking about methodology at all, and not just speculating about our unconscious 'habits of thought'.

But, with *this* interpretation, (II) is absurd! And we don't need to get involved in the big argument about 'general laws in history' to see that (II) is absurd! Let us stick to the subject we have discussed so much in these lectures, the subject of *translation*.

I have been studying Hebrew recently. So I take it as something we know that *shemen* means oil. (Quine would deny that this is part of *knowledge*, but he is almost alone in this.) Can this piece of knowledge be checked 'scientifically' in Mill's or Nagel's sense?

Since one way of checking the statement is to *ask bilinguals*, and there are plenty of Hebrew-English bilinguals, there would seem to be no problem. Just ask 100 (or 1,000, or whatever) bilinguals. *But how do the bilinguals know?* (*Do they really know?* – a peculiar kind of scepticism.)

If I want to avoid using bilinguals, I can just learn Hebrew myself (ideally, by direct method, in Israel – not relying on explanations in English). But how do I check what I think I am learning?

Well, if I go to a gas station, and say *bedok et hashemen* and the attendant punches me in the nose (and the same thing happens at other gas stations) my faith in my translation of *bedok et hashemen* as 'check the oil' will be shaken. But notice what is going on! I am assuming (1) the attendant wants to sell gas and oil; (2) it is not *obligatory* in Israel to say 'bevakasha' (*please*) when making a request; (3) if someone wants to sell oil, and a customer asks 'check the oil' in the language of the seller (and no obligatory politeness-rules have been violated) the seller will check the oil (or, perhaps, say 'I'm out of oil' in his language, or – rarely – 'I'm too busy', but *not* punch the customer in the nose); (4) someone driving up to a gas station will be treated as a customer. Each time I check my 'analytical hypothesis' (i.e. my translation skills) in a new context, a *new* list of psychological/sociological hypotheses of the order of (1)–(4) will be imported from 'general background knowledge', or whatever. The whole list of such things that I use and believe cannot, obviously, be *written down* in advance.

Oddly enough (since all this should be grist for his mill) Quine over-simplifies all this with his notion of 'stimulus meaning'. On his account, only contexts in which *I* utter a sentence and the Hebrew speaker says *yes* (*ken*) or *no* (*lo*) matter. But in fact, even if an analytical hypothesis were to fit *those* situations perfectly, it is at least logically possible that it would break down completely when I used it 'on the street' (or in the gas station), i.e. tried to conduct a conversation or 'make sense' of conversations I overheard – and this is surely the test we care about.

Moral: testing the 'hypothesis that *shemen* means *oil*' involves testing the *conjunction* of an 'analytical hypothesis' *I can't state* properly (as the failure of mechanical translation shows) and psychological premises I obviously can't list in advance!

In fine, knowledge of such a *simple* fact as '*shemen* means oil' cannot be justified/confirmed by following the paradigms of inductive logic. Perhaps the inferences we are making could be put in paradigmatic form by a Martian (or a Laplacian super-mind) – but *humans* can't (practically, and maybe not even 'in principle') make such inferences explicit. We have to rely on: 'Well, I have learned to understand Hebrew (or whatever language), and I am sure my understanding is right, because I can talk to the people and understand their answers.'

But this knowledge that one *is* 'talking to the people and understanding their answers' is typical *practical* knowledge. The inferences are not, in any *serious* non-trivial sense, *scientific* inferences (except, *maybe*, 'unconsciously'), and the key terms – 'means', 'understand' – cannot, as I have argued, be made scientifically precise.

It seems to me that a certain version of scientism in the social sciences collapses right here. The idea that what we *know* is co-extensive with what we can check 'publicly' following well-understood paradigms of scientific testing does not even fit some of the *simplest* facts we know, such as the meaning of the words in a foreign language.

(Maybe this is the real reason Quine believes in the indeterminacy of translation: since this knowledge doesn't belong to 'science' in the logical empiricist sense, it isn't knowledge, in his view.)

DIGRESSION ON THE CONSENSUS CRITERION

Part of the doctrine that the logical empiricists pushed is that *knowledge = public knowledge*. If this means that what is known can be agreed upon by all competent people (almost all? – *all* is awfully strict!) who study the subject (where competence is measured in terms of certain skills – depending on the area), then the '*shemen*-means-oil' example is an example of *public* knowledge that does not employ the paradigms of inductive logic in any explicit way (and can't do so, practically speaking). On the other hand, in the Middle Ages scholastic philosophy would have also been 'public' by this criterion (consensus of the competent).

If 'knowledge = public knowledge' means, on the other hand, that *ideally rational* people would all agree, then it's awfully vague. 'People who follow the paradigms of inductive logic intelligently would all agree?' I have argued that these *can't be* applied (explicitly) to this sort of subject matter. In any case, it is *not* a necessary truth that ideally rational people would all agree about knowledge. I *know* I had cereal for breakfast this morning. Suppose I'm a well-known liar. Then maybe ideally rational people wouldn't accept my say-so. Maybe they couldn't know if I had cereal or not. But I *still* know.

PRACTICAL KNOWLEDGE

What is the *source* of the fact that we have knowledge (even *public* knowledge, as we have just seen) – that cannot be 'scientized' – 'verified' by a verification that publicly conforms to the criteria of 'scientific methodology'? One source is clearly this: that we can acquire *skills* that are too complex to describe by a theory. I can learn to translate from one language to another. But I cannot describe the skill I have acquired by an (explicit) theory. Maybe my *brain* has a theory. Given that language has a discrete structure, my brain must employ something like algorithms – although I don't think algorithms are *all* that is involved, even in translation. But even if my brain has a complete 'analytical hypothesis' all 'written out' in some hypothetical 'brain language', *I* don't and scientists today don't. The key fact is that *skills* don't always depend on *theories* (as the example of *walking* already illustrates). And knowledge – even verbalized knowledge – can be embodied in a *skill* and not a theory.

Ordinary psychological explanations are another example of the same phenomenon. It may be perfectly clear to everyone in a given situation that Jones is jealous of Smith's reputation. But one couldn't give *anything like* a 'scientific proof' that Jones is jealous of Smith's reputation. It isn't, for example, that 'Jones said blah-blah and people who say blah-blah are generally jealous'. Even if it is true that people who say blah-blah are generally jealous, one can easily envisage *an indefinite number* of situations in which someone might say blah-blah and *not* be jealous. So it is more like 'people who say blah-blah are likely to be jealous *unless special circumstances obtain* and no special circumstances obtained in this instance' (a *ceteris paribus* inference, like the practical syllogism). The case is like the translation case in that one can't 'verify' *Jones is jealous* in isolation: one would have to verify a *huge* 'psychological theory' which covered all the 'special circumstances'. And this, of course, is *implicit* in our knowledge of people, and our *ability* to use psychological descriptions – not something we can state explicitly. Again, it is a feature of 'scientific' knowledge (at least if we take *physics* as the paradigm) that we *use measuring instruments that we understand.* Our theory applies to our measuring instruments, and to their interactions with what they are used to measure, not just to the objects we measure. It is a feature of *practical* knowledge that we often have to use *ourselves* (or other people) as the measuring instruments – and we do *not* have an explicit theory of *these* interactions.

PHYSICS AND LOGIC

Even in physics, however, the situation is not so simple. What the theory actually describes is (typically) an idealized 'closed system'. The theory of this 'closed system' can be as precise as you want. And it is *within* this idealization that one gets the familiar examples of the 'scientific method'. But the *application* of physics depends on the fact that we can produce in the laboratory, or find in the world, *open* systems which approximate to the idealized system sufficiently well for the theory to yield very accurate predictions. The decision that conditions have been approximated well in a given case – that it is even *worthwhile* to apply the idealized model to *this* case – typically depends on unformalized practical knowledge. The moral is that the so-called 'scientific method' ('SM') is only a formalization of *some aspects* of scientific methodology. Physics *itself* could not proceed using *only* the 'SM'.

The distinction between knowledge obtained by the 'SM' and practical knowledge is not, then, the same as the cut between *science* and other kinds of *knowledge*. Some 'non-scientific knowledge' is *presupposed* by science. For example, I have been arguing that 'refers' and 'true' (i.e. refers-in-L and true-in-L for variable L) cannot be made 'scientifically precise'. Yet *truth* is a fundamental term in *logic* – a *precise science*!

Again, any historian or sociologist has to rely on *translations* of foreign documents – hence on knowledge *not* checked (or checkable, at least not practically speaking) by the 'SM'. But more than that: if a historian reads documents, examines the public actions, reads the diaries and letters, how then does he decide 'Smith was hungry for power'? *Not* by applying 'general laws of history, sociology, and psychology' to the data as positivist methodologists urge he should! Rather he has to absorb all this material, and then *rely on his human wisdom* that this shows power-hunger 'beyond a reasonable doubt' (as the courts say). In effect, he uses *himself* as a 'measuring instrument'; which is pretty much what Weber, Dilthey, etc., urged (I'll say more about *Verstehen* later). Sometimes his decision is controversial (even when he is right), but sometimes not (does anyone doubt that *Nero* was egotistical?).

What I have just pointed out is, of course, a similarity between knowledge in physics and in the social sciences – both depend on unformalized practical knowledge – what Polanyi calls 'implicit knowledge'. But the similarity rests on and presupposes a *difference*. I argued in the previous lecture that although we do sometimes succeed in constructing good explanatory models of some natural kinds in physics, it is hopeless to seek an *explanatory model* of the natural kind 'human being' (although we may, of course, discover empirical regularities and perhaps even *laws* about human beings). This is what accounts for the *unformalizability* of practical knowledge.

SOME PSYCHOLOGICAL QUESTIONS

Now I want to digress on some psychological questions:

Consider the case of figuring out how to climb a mountain by 'climbing it in one's head'. What this strongly suggests is that a lot of the information we have available to us may not be *stored* in propositional form. We can *put* the relevant considerations into words; but that doesn't mean that it was written out in 'brain code'. (In fact, there are a number of experiments that strongly suggest that the brain stores *images*.) I'm not suggesting that the brain is an 'analogue' as opposed to a 'digital' machine; I'm suggesting that it's *neither*. On any plausible theory, the brain has digital aspects (something like computation almost certainly goes on); but it may well process a considerable amount of non-digital information. In particular, *translation* need not be 'mechanical' in all its aspects. It may be that we sometimes match pictures to the situations we are in, in order to find the 'frame' to use in translation. In this case testing our translation-abilities wouldn't be testing a *theory* at all – even an 'unconscious' one; and similarly for our psychological-explanation-abilities and even our ordinary-language-material-object-explanation-abilities.

Second, some of our ability to *picture* how people are likely to respond may well be *innate*. Indeed, our disposition to *believe what other people tell us* could hardly be the product of an inference – otherwise, as John McDowell remarks, we would not be justified in saying we *know* what we have learned from other people. (If it's an inference it isn't that good.) But the disposition to believe what one is told is both a special case of *Verstehen* and fundamental to all knowledge – not just social knowledge! Physics may rest on *Verstehen* as much as the social sciences.

VERSTEHEN

Now, what the critics of *Verstehen* say is that 'putting oneself in someone else's place' may be a useful source of *hypotheses* but such hypotheses still have to be *confirmed* (using the 'SM'). Part of this I have now criticized: *checking* such hypotheses isn't done using (explicitly, paradigmatically) the 'SM' – and maybe not even 'unconsciously' (although that's a question more for cognitive psychology than for methodology). Let me discuss the other part: the contention that *Verstehen* belongs to the 'context of discovery' and not to the 'context of justification'. Let me grant that what we 'know' by empathy needs to be checked, and so is not *knowledge*. It doesn't follow that it is *only* 'hypothesis'. It is accepted doctrine in Philosophy of Science that inductive testing of theories presupposes some *a priori* (in the sense of antecedent) weighting of the theories – a weighting *prior* to the checking. In probability theories of confirmation (theories based on Bayes's theorem) this would be a 'prior probability distribution'; in elimination theories it would be a 'simplicity ordering'. (Popper thinks one can just use a 'content measure', but that doesn't work at all.) I'll speak of a 'prior probability' here, although I myself think this is only qualitative, not numerical.

It is also accepted that no one has been able to *formalize* the intuitive judgments of scientists which *in practice* constitute the 'prior probability metric'.

Now, what I want to suggest is that empathy may give less than 'Knowledge' (with a capital K), but it gives more than mere logical or physical possibility. It gives *plausibility* – it is the source of prior probability in many judgments about people. To revive Platonic terminology, it may not provide 'knowledge', but it does provide 'right opinion' – and I am arguing that knowledge *depends on* a good deal of right opinion.

It seems to me that this is all that an intelligent defender of *Verstehen* in the social sciences has to defend against Nagel *et al*. *Verstehen* is a source of *prior probability*; the 'hypothesis' to which we assign significantly high prior probability on the basis of '*Verstehen*' (empathy) must indeed be 'checked', but *even this checking is ultimately intuitive*. The alternative picture of social science – as based on 'general laws of history, sociology and psychology', confirmed by the 'SM', and applied to data as in physics – is false to present social science and utopian as a vision of future social science.

The purpose of Nagel *et al*. was to rule out what they viewed as 'obscurantism' and 'metaphysics' in the social sciences. Worthy as these aims are, to pursue them by misrepresenting what actually goes on is to promulgate an ideology, in the pejorative sense of 'ideology'; not to promote clarity of method.

RECOMMENDATIONS?

Many social scientists, and many who are not social scientists, may be impatient with what I have said. 'Very well,' they may want to reply, 'you have convinced us that the social sciences cannot realistically aim at the sort of detailed mathematical model of their subject matter that physicists try to construct of theirs; and that intuitive and unformalized knowledge of various kinds will remain indispensable. But what do you recommend in place of the image of the social sciences becoming more like physical science?' This question springs from the very real fact that sociology, in particular, found at the end of the nineteenth century that it was becoming increasingly hard to attain to any kind of objectivity at all, and the fact that even today historians and political scientists have to face and cope with the charge 'that's just *your* interpretation'. Without a standard of objectivity provided by the imitation of physics, what are we to do?

It is true that empiricist methodology was meant to lead us out of the darkness of disagreement and controversy. But sometimes, when one has taken a wrong path, the best way out of a dark forest involves re-entering it. I do not know what glories social science may attain in the future (although I see no reason to doubt that intelligence, imagination, and sensitivity will produce masterpieces in the future in this area as they have in others). But I do know that 'scientizing' the social sciences (a barbarous term I have invented to fit a barbarous idea) is a confusion and a source of confusion.

If I have at last *no* specific recommendation to make to social scientists – to students of social and human phenomena, rather – still, I have some misunderstandings to forestall. I am *not* saying that mathematics has no place in social science. Mathematical economics hardly presents us with a mathematical model of a whole person; but what it does is still of value. I am not saying testable theories have no place, or that statistics have no place, or even that the 'SM' has no place. My view is rather a pluralist one. All these have their place and we should use them when and where we can. But these techniques have no shortage of defenders. The purpose of this lecture was to redress the balance by asserting the claims of that vast fund of unformalized and unformalizable knowledge of man upon which we depend and with which we live and breathe and have our being every day of our lives.

If the point of view I am advocating became accepted there would surely be a greater acceptance of both diversity and continuity in social and human studies – continuity and diversity between empirical studies in sociology, for example, and history (no longer conceived of as consisting of 'laws' and 'initial conditions'); and continuity and diversity between history and sociology, on the one hand, and the political or cultural essay on the other. The social sciences might become, in part, more 'literary' – some books might even be written well! There would also be less concern to find a methodological rule that would settle controversies and produce consensus. Indeed, on some questions the only consensus to be obtained is the consensus of the wise.

Should we *regret* the fact that the social sciences cannot realistically hope to resemble physical science? To ask this is to ask if we should regret the fact that we cannot understand ourselves and each other as the physicist understands the harmonic oscillator (nor – what is surely very different – the way God might see us). If we are doomed to have neither a computer's-eye view nor a God's-eye view of ourselves and each other, is that such a terrible fate? We are men and women; and men and women we may be lucky enough to remain. Let us try to preserve our humanity by, among other things, taking a humane view of ourselves and our self-knowledge.

NOTES

Lecture I

1 Cf. Tarski's 'The Concept of Truth in Formalized Languages', reprinted in his *Logic, Semantics, Metamathematics,* Oxford University Press, 1956, pp. 152–278.

2 In logic a definition is called 'explicit' if it provides a rule for *eliminating* the defined expression – replacing it with primitive vocabulary – in all contexts. So-called 'inductive' definitions are not really definitions at all, in this sense, but rather are specifications of the extension of a notion by a mathematical induction – in this case, an induction on the number of logical connectives in the predicate. But such inductive definitions can be *turned into* explicit definitions, by more or less complicated devices from mathematical logic.

3 Such a language is called *monadic* (because only one-place predicates occur) and *uniform* (because no quantifier is in the scope of any other quantifier). The latter restriction is inessential – any monadic formula is equivalent to a *uniform* monadic formula (see W. V. Quine's *Methods of Logic*, 3rd edn, New York, Holt, 1967, part II, for a proof); but the restriction to *monadic* formulas only is essential if the full complication of Tarski's theory (the use of infinite sequences, etc.) is to be avoided; and I wish to avoid it here for expository purposes.

4 For a fuller discussion of this point, see my *Philosophy of Logic,* New York, Harper & Row, 1971, pp. 18–21.

5 Cf. Field's 'Tarski's Theory of Truth', *Journal of Philosophy*, vol. 69, no. 13 (1972), pp. 347–75.

6 *Ibid.*, pp. 362–3.

Lecture II

1 It will emerge that I think that realism is *like* an empirical hypothesis in that (1) it could be false, and (2) facts are relevant to its support (or to

78

criticizing it); but that doesn't mean that realism is *scientific* (in any standard sense of 'scientific') or that realism is a *hypothesis*. The notion 'scientific' will be discussed later in these lectures. In previous papers I have discussed why belief in an external world and in other minds is not a 'hypothesis'. (See Chs 1 and 17 of my *Mind, Language, and Reality; Philosophical Papers,* vol. 2, Cambridge University Press, 1975.)

2 *Realism and Scientific Epistemology,* Cambridge University Press, forthcoming.

3 In 'What Theories are Not', reprinted in my *Mathematics, Matter, and Method; Philosophical Papers,* vol. 1, Cambridge University Press, 1975.

4 In 'Language and Reality', in my *Mind, Language, and Reality; Philosophical Papers,* vol. 2, Cambridge University Press, 1975.

5 This was pointed out by Kurt Gödel in 'On Intuitionistic Arithmetic and Number Theory', reprinted in Martin Davis (ed.), *The Undecidable,* New York, Raven Press, 1965.

6 One problem with reformulating physics intuitionistically is that one cannot state laws such as Newton's Law of Gravity which assert that two different empirically given real numbers (the force of A on B, and the quotient of g times the product of the masses and the distance squared) are exactly equal in intuitionist mathematics. (Cf. my paper 'What is Mathematical Truth?', in *Mathematics, Matter and Method; Philosophical Papers,* vol. 1, Cambridge University Press, 1975, for an explanation.) But one *can* say that such a law holds to, say, thirty decimal places – and, if one doesn't expect the law to be retained in the long run anyway, and isn't trying to 'converge' by successive approximations to anything which is objectively *true,* then one presumably wouldn't mind *weakening* physical theory to this extent.

Lecture III

1 'The Logic of Quantum Mechanics', in my *Mathematics, Matter and Method; Philosophical Papers,* vol. 1, Cambridge University Press, 1975.

2 'The Meaning of "Meaning"', in my *Mind, Language, and Reality; Philosophical Papers,* vol. 2, Cambridge University Press, 1975.

3 A. Garfinkel, *Explanation and Individuals,* Yale University Press, forthcoming.

4 A Martian friend of mine has suggested that 'rabbitscape' would capture the Martian way of thinking better than the somewhat stilted 'undetached rabbit-part'.

Lecture IV

1 Nor is it necessarily the case that the native (e.g. Karl) could help us if he would. After all, the 'native speaker' of number theory cannot 'tell us' what number words *refer to* (as Frege complained); *we* have to decide, from the vantage point of *our* language. (Suppose we had *only* set talk and

no number vocabulary, and encountered for the first time a culture that spoke of 'numbers'.) Why should it not happen that Karl, after learning *both* English and Martian, says to us 'When you force me to think about the problem, it seems to me that *"gavagai"* is, in a way, *ambiguous* – I can *construe* gavagais as being rabbits or I can construe them as being undetached rabbit-parts. But Gavagese isn't ambiguous from within; I just think of gavagais as gavagais'?

2 A Turing Machine is a finite state automaton with a potentially infinite memory (in the form of a two-way potentially infinite paper tape, on which the machine may print or erase, and which the machine may move right or left). The use of automaton models in the philosophy of mind is discussed in a number of my papers in *Mind, Language and Reality; Philosophical Papers,* vol. 2, Cambridge University Press, 1975. For a general discussion, see in particular the papers titled 'The Nature of Mental States', and 'Philosophy and our Mental Life', in that volume.

3 Cf. his paper 'Meaning', *Philosophical Review*, vol. LXVI, no. 3 (1957), pp. 377–86.

4 Cf. his book *Meaning*, New York, Oxford University Press, 1972.

5 H. L. A. Hart and A. M. Honore, *Causation in the Law*, Oxford University Press, 1959.

Lecture V

1 Kripke's views were presented in talks at Princeton, reprinted as 'Naming and Necessity' in D. Davidson and G. Harman (eds), *Semantics of Natural Language,* Dordrecht, Reidel, 1972.

2 Cf. 'Explanation and Reference', and 'The Meaning of "Meaning"', reprinted in my *Mind, Language and Reality; Philosophical Papers,* vol. 2, Cambridge University Press, 1975.

Lecture VI

1 In *A System of Logic.* The words quoted are the opening words of Book VI (8th edn, New York, 1881).

2 Edgar Zilsel, 'Physics and the Problem of Historico-Sociological Laws', in H. Feigl and M. Brodbeck (eds), *Readings in the Philosophy of Science*, New York, Appleton-Century-Crofts, 1953, pp. 714–22.

3 *Ibid.,* p. 714.

4 Ernest Nagel, 'The Logic of Historical Analysis', in H. Feigl and M. Brodbeck (eds), *Readings in the Philosophy of Science,* New York, Appleton-Century-Crofts, 1953, pp. 688–700.

5 *Ibid.,* p. 700.

PART TWO

LITERATURE, SCIENCE, AND REFLECTION *

LITERATURE, SCIENCE, AND REFLECTION *

Although my intention is to discuss the relation of literary and scientific ways of thinking to what may properly be called human understanding, for reasons that will become clear shortly I shall begin by saying something about the branch of my own subject called moral philosophy. What I will say about moral philosophy is strongly influenced by some recent, and unfortunately still unpublished, work by Judy Baker and Paul Grice. Grice and Baker take the question to be the simple three-word question 'how to live'. I like this starting point, not only because it seems fresh and unhackneyed in comparison with the usual academic ways of beginning the investigation of ethical topics, but because it has the effect of making ethics at once a branch of practical knowledge, and I think that this is a very important idea.

However, can one rationally discuss the question 'how to live'? Of course, someone who has a morality, at least in the sense of having arrived at a 'style' or set of habits of life, and even some-one who has reflected on his style of life, and who is conscious of having what we call a character, and who accepts or thinks he ought to accept certain kinds of criticism of his character, e.g. that he is being irrational or stupid in his choice of means to certain ends, may reject any more fundamental criticism of his own morality or character by simply saying 'well, that's how I feel like living' or 'this way of living suits me'. If most people blocked any but the most superficial means-ends criticism in this way, such an institution as morality would not and could not ever arise.

It seems to me to be a very important psychological fact, although unfortunately not the sort of fact that psychologists very often talk about, that people reflect on their own character and also that people generally try to justify their character to other people, at least when it is criticized. We are, most of us, interested in justifying at least some features of our own style of life, in the sense of giving a defence of them that would appeal to others as a justification. Of course, there are limits to this. As Baker and Grice also point out, we want not only to have a morality of wide appeal, we want at the same time to have a morality that leaves us plenty of 'discretionary space'. A morality that dictated a duty to us in every conceivable circumstance would be unlivable.

Yet the fact is that once we see that moral reasoning does not take place in a Cartesian vacuum, that it takes place in the context of people trying to answer criticisms of their character, and in the context of people trying to justify ways of life to other people, trying to criticize the ways of life of other people, etc., by producing reasons that have some kind of general appeal, we see that the question of the objectivity of ethics arises in an entirely new way or appears in an entirely new light. The question whether there is one objectively best morality or a number of objectively best moralities which, hopefully, agree on a good many principles or in a good many cases, is simply the question whether, given the desiderata that automatically arise once we undertake the enterprise of giving a justification of principles for living which will be of *general* appeal, then, will it turn out that these desiderata select a best morality or a group of moralities which have a significant measure of agreement on a number of significant questions.

In a terminology employed by John Rawls, the question is whether there is such a group of moralities or a single morality which can survive the test of 'wide reflective equilibrium'. In fact, one might view what Grice and Baker are doing as trying to work out a detailed description of the process of 'arriving at reflective equilibrium'.

Notice, by the way, that practical knowledge is not scientific knowledge; but that is not to say that practical knowledge is some kind of transcendental knowledge. There is nothing obscure about what it is in the case of practical knowledge that 'transcends' rigorous scientific theorizing or formalization at the present time. The reason that knowledge of, say, *wines* or *cooking* is not scientific knowledge is that the criterion of successful cooking or of a successful wine is a satisfied human palate – and not just any palate, at that. The question whether good cooking or good wine making could be reduced to a science 'in principle' is an uninteresting one, because 'in principle' has nothing to do with actual human life in the foreseeable future. To be sure, it is not 'logically impossible' that someday we might have so complete a theory of our own nature that we could program a computer to determine what would and would not satisfy us. But, if that ever comes to be the case, then it cannot but alter our nature itself. If we ever become so transparent to ourselves that the distinction between practical knowledge and theoretical knowledge disappears, then no doubt such institutions as science, philosophy, and literature may well disappear in their present forms too. And if one cannot reduce cooking well or making wine well to a 'science', then how much less can one hope to reduce *living* well to a 'science'!

Yet the fact that one cannot reduce living well to a science does not mean that reflecting on how to live well is not a rational enterprise, or that there cannot be any objective knowledge about it. Incidentally, science itself involves practical as well as theoretical knowledge; although particular scientific theories are the very paradigm of theoretical knowledge, knowing how to make good scientific theories is unlikely to be a theoretical science in the foreseeable future.

To emphasize the point again: my answer to the question whether morality can 'in principle' be a science is that it can only be a science when, if ever, human nature is totally scientifically transparent to humans. Since that will not happen for a millennium, if ever, the question about morality being a science is best put aside.

One point that Baker and Grice make which is of importance to my present topic is that the role of imagination in practical reasoning has been systematically ignored or downplayed by the philosophical tradition. One of their examples is a very simple one, but all the more instructive for that reason. A man is climbing a mountain. Halfway up he stops, because he is unsure how to go on. He imagines himself continuing via one route.

In his imagination, he proceeds on up to a certain point, and then he gets into a difficulty which he cannot, in his imagination, see how to get out of. He then imagines himself going up by a different route. This time he is able to imagine himself getting all the way to the top without difficulty. So he takes the second route.

The point is that this may be a perfectly rational way to solve a practical problem, and yet this sort of reasoning need not at all be reducible to any kind of linear proposition-by-proposition reasoning. The mountain climber is, so to speak, functioning as an analogue computer rather than a digital computer when he solves his problem by 'unreeling' in his imagination, as vividly as possible, exactly 'what would happen if. . . .' Of course, saying that this is not linear propositional reasoning is not to deny that *after* he has imagined 'what would happen if . . .' he can *put* the relevant considerations into words. It is to say that he need not have *stored* the relevant information *in the form of words*. Grice and Baker suggest that imagining ways of living, or particular aspects of ways of living, is tremendously important in moral argument and in practical argument generally; and that 'rhetoric' need not be a mere propaganda device, as it is generally viewed, but may be a legitimate instrument for the purpose of getting someone to imagine *vividly* what it would be like to live one way rather than another, or at least it may be a way of getting him or her to see vividly what the *appeal* of one morality is as opposed to the appeal of another.

What I like about the Grice and Baker approach is that it suggests that moral reasoning may be reasoning in the full sense of the word, while at the same time suggesting that it is something which involves not just the logical faculties, in the narrow sense, but our full capacity to imagine and feel, in short, our full sensibility.

It is at this point that I want to discuss literature. Literature has for a long time refused to be, or to be primarily, propaganda for any morality, or philosophy, or ideology. Lady Murisaki, writing in tenth-century Japan, rejects the idea that moral uplift is the purpose of literature just as wholeheartedly as any novelist would today. What literature does is not the same as what moral or ideological rhetoric does. Literature does not, usually, enable us to visualize *ideal* ways of life. Literature does not, or does not often, depict *solutions*. What especially the novel does is aid us in the imaginative re-creation of moral perplexities, in the widest sense. (I don't contend that this is what is aesthetically valuable about novels; indeed, I shall not deal with questions of aesthetic value at all. But I contend that this is an important fact about the novel as it has developed in the last few centuries.) Sometimes it is said that literature describes 'the human predicament', which is perhaps a way of referring to this. But the pomposity of the phrase obscures the point. The important point is not that there is some *one* predicament which is *the* human predicament, and which literature sometimes describes; the point is that for *many* reasons it seems increasingly difficult to imagine *any* way of life which is both at all ideal and feasible; and literature often puts before us both extremely vividly and in extremely rich emotional detail why and how this seems to be so in different societies, in different times, and from different perspectives. I want to suggest that if moral reasoning, at the reflective level, is the conscious criticism of ways of life, then the sensitive appreciation in the imagination of predicaments and perplexities must be essential to sensitive moral reasoning. Novels and plays do not set moral knowledge before us, that is true. But they do (frequently) do something for us that must be done for us if we are to gain any moral knowledge.

In a world in which revealed books no longer command general acceptance, very few people would deny that scientific knowledge must play some role in the resolution of moral problems on both a social and an individual level. But it is easy to be puzzled about what role literature can and should play. At the same time, the social and psychological sciences tend to disappoint us. Thus we tend to be at once disillusioned with science and unclear as to the bearing of literature. I suggest that until we arrive at a better view of moral reasoning than we have recently been fed, we will not be able to arrive at any kind of reasoned consensus as to what either literature or the sciences can contribute to our deepest concerns.

While our disillusionment with science, from the point of view of moral and broadly human and social problems, is understandable, there is a case against science which I have heard argued by some of my humanistic colleagues which seems to me fundamentally misguided.

I once heard a group of fellow teachers of the humanities at a Christian Gauss seminar at Princeton break into a discussion of scientists. The consensus was that scientists are ignorant clods who never read anything more literary than the latest number of *Galaxy*. A number of speakers added that scientists are cocksure even outside (*especially* outside) of their professional specialities, and that scientists are socially dangerous because they think that they are in an especially good position to advise governments, and because governments are likely to be overawed by their scientific credentials and to take their advice on policy matters. This last – the advice on policy matters – was characterized as 'simplistic'.

The humanists saw nothing odd about characterizing *themselves* as 'cautious', 'aware of the complexity of things', etc., even though *humanistic* intellectuals in the present century have jumped on the following bandwagons in significant numbers: psychoanalysis; Existentialism (this is true for continental intellectuals); and something vaguely described (by Paul Goodman, Norman Mailer, Kenneth Tynan *et al.*) as 'sexual revolution'. What scientist worthy of the name has been willing to say flatly that *all* dreams are 'wish fulfilments'? That all human life is meaningless, except in so far as one gives it meaning by a completely *arbitrary* act of 'commitment'? That we need a total (and totally undescribed) 'sexual revolution'? Humanists are all too willing to remember that these pronouncements are the pronouncements of a minority in their ranks, and to forget that the wild pronouncements on matters of public policy that have come from scientists are the pronouncements of an equally small minority of the scientific community. Of course, both scientists and humanists have at times been guilty of supporting various kinds of discrimination, colonialism, etc.; and both scientists and humanists have spoken out for decency.

Fortunately for my present purposes, most of this 'case' does not need discussing, consisting as it does of prejudiced opinions about scientists which would not be terribly relevant to the value or nature of science even if they happened to be correct. What is of interest is the claim that, so to speak, Euripides, Freud, and Dostoevsky are 'all ye know on earth and all ye need to know'.

It is hard to know what to say here, because, putting aside the difficult question of the validity of psychoanalysis, one grants that *Medea* and *The Brothers Karamazov* are great and moving works of art. We are above all human beings, and these works do move us as human beings. But why should placing a high value on art be incompatible with placing a high value on science, and a high value on yet other good things besides?

We get closer to the real issue if we realize that according to some – according to the thinkers I wish to criticize – the value of, say, Dostoevsky, is not purely aesthetic in the way in which the value of an abstract painting is, or is sometimes supposed to be, purely aesthetic. The Greek dramatists, Freudian psychology, and the Russian novel are all supposed by these thinkers to embody *knowledge – knowledge about man*. Thus they both do and do not conflict with science. They conflict with science in the sense of representing a rival kind of knowledge, and thereby contest the claim of science to monopolize reliable knowledge. But it is a rival *kind* of knowledge, and hence inaccessible to scientific testing. If we add the claim that this rival kind of knowledge is somehow 'higher' or more important than scientific knowledge, we have a full-blown obscurantist position – not the position of the serious student or critic of literature, to be sure, but the position of the religion of literature.

I don't mean to suggest that there is nothing at all that the proponents of this view are on to; but discussion of the view at once gets embroiled with thorny and difficult issues. The following remarks on the way in which, say, the novel does and does not embody 'knowledge of man' are offered with some diffidence.

It seems to me wrong either to say that novels give knowledge of man or to say categorically that they do not. The situation is more complicated than a single simple affirmation on either side can suggest. No matter how profound the psychological insights of a novelist may seem to be, they cannot be called *knowledge* if they have not been tested. To say that the perceptive reader can just *see* that the psychological insights of a novelist are not just plausible, but that they have some kind of universal truth, is to return to the idea of knowledge by intuition about matters of empirical fact, to The Method of What is Agreeable to Reason. To take some examples of novels less difficult than Dostoevsky's: if I read Celine's *Journey to the End of the Night* I do not *learn* that love does not exist, that all human beings are hateful and hating (even if – and I am sure this is not the case – those propositions should be true). What I learn is to see the world as it looks to someone who is sure that hypothesis is correct. I see what plausibility that hypothesis has; what it would be like if it *were* true; how someone could possibly think that it *is* true. But all this is still not empirical knowledge. Yet it is not correct to say that it is not knowledge at all; for being aware of a new interpretation of the facts, however repellent, of a construction that can – I now see – be put upon the facts, however perversely – is a kind of knowledge. It is knowledge of a possibility. It is *conceptual* knowledge.

It may seem strange to describe something as real and 'empirical' as a vision of how humans behave and of what 'makes them tick' as *conceptual* knowledge; but that is all it is unless it is tested, if not scientifically, at least tested in the actual experience of intelligent and sensitive men and women. Thinking of a hypothesis that one had not considered before is *conceptual* discovery; it is not empirical discovery, although it may result in empirical discovery if the hypothesis turns out to be correct. Yet the 'knowledge of a possibility' that literature gives us should not be knowledge of a *mere* possibility. That the possibility Celine holds before us *is* a 'mere' possibility is, after all, one of the reasons we do not rate Celine higher than we do as a novelist. So again the situation is complicated, there are both empirical and conceptual elements in the knowledge we gain from literature.

But, it may be objected, the novelist's 'hypothesis' is not subject to scientific testing. It is not that *sort* of hypothesis. This is often, but not always, true. If Celine were right – if all apparent instances of love were really disguised self-interest of the most selfish kind – I have little doubt that one could find empirical evidence for this of many kinds. Perhaps the difficulty here is that operationists have convinced too many people that all scientific hypotheses bear their testability on their face, and hence that any statement that it is not obvious how to test cannot be in the sphere of science at all. But this is a gross caricature of science, even if it is one that many scientists have been taught to believe. Very often the genius of a scientist lies precisely in thinking of a way of testing a statement that did not seem testable at all.

To take a different, and more plausible, example than Celine: it is one of the virtues of *The Golden Notebook* that it presents an extremely plausible account of how it felt to be a communist in the 1940s. Yet it cannot be said that after reading it one has acquired *knowledge* of what it was like to be a communist in the 1940s, unless one has some independent source of knowledge that Doris Lessing's account is factually true. You may feel convinced upon reading *The Golden Notebook*; you may say to yourself *this is what it must have been like*; but unless you want to substitute subjective plausibility and conformity with What is Agreeable to Reason for answering to the objective facts and being shown by adequate evidence to so answer as the criteria for 'knowledge', you have no right to say 'I *know* that this is what it was like'. You do not *know*; and the very next week you may be convinced by an equally plausible novel that it must have all been entirely different from Doris Lessing's description.

There is, however, something Doris Lessing does in *The Golden Notebook* which is very important and whose value does not depend on the correctness or incorrectness of her description of the British Communist Party (although it does depend on the correctness of her description of how that Party was perceived, and on the correctness of part of her criticism of the communists – that they were totalitarian and manipulative, for example). She represents to us a certain moral perplexity, a problem or a group of moral problems, some of them connected with being a woman in the present century, some of them connected with being a person with a social conscience in the present century, as that moral perplexity might have been felt by one perfectly possible person in a perfectly definite period. What I am suggesting is that if we want to reason rationally about feminism, communism, liberalism, or just about life in the twentieth century, then what Doris Lessing does for our sensibility is enormously important.

To think of the novel itself as presenting us with some kind of nonscientific knowledge of man is making it all somehow too much like *propositions*. I said at the outset that there is a sense in which there is such a thing as 'nonscientific knowledge of man'; moral knowledge, if not 'nonscientific knowledge of man' in the sense of the people just alluded to, is practical knowledge of how to live; and practical knowledge is not 'scientific' in the sense of being theoretical knowledge. Moreover, practical knowledge, as we saw earlier, involves our full capacities of feeling and imagination. What the people I described were, I think, right about is that literature somehow ties up with a kind of knowledge which is close to the centre of moral concern and which is not 'scientific knowledge' in any reasonably standard sense. But saying that literature 'gives' nonscientific knowledge of man makes the matter too simple.

Just as some thinkers tend to view literature as knowledge, so today other thinkers tend to view science as a philosophy. The tendency to view science as a philosophy is an understandable one. Many traditional philosophical questions – for example, the infinity of space and time, and the nature of space, time, and matter – have been abandoned to physics, by most realistically minded philosophers. At most, the professional philosopher hopes to be able to clarify the results the physicist obtains. The social sciences are, for many reasons, in a less impressive state than the physical sciences; but here there is already the hope if not the achievement – the hope that social and psychological science may one day shed some real light on the nature of society and man. Certainly few philosophers from any perspective would today write about justice without considering the bearing of economic theory, or about the parts of the psyche without considering psychological theory. But if science is a philosophy, it suffers from being all metaphysics and no ethics; and metaphysics without ethics is blind. Social science often seems sterile precisely because it is interested in the mere description of what we have in the way of society now, and not in the possibility of a society which is at once feasible and just; and psychological science rarely discusses man in society, or the possibility, in *any* society, of ways of life which are at once moral, feasible, and rewarding.

I am not urging that science should be pursued only for practical ends or only for moral enlightenment. Of course, knowledge for its own sake is and should be a 'terminal value' for educated men and women. But I contend that even the *philosophical* significance of science, let alone the practical significance, becomes hard to see without distortion when science and moral reflection are as sharply separated as they have become in our culture.

Relativity theory bears on the nature of matter, space, and time, to be sure; but it also bears on the whole nature and possibility of human certainty, for example. The overthrow of

Euclidean geometry was not *just* the overthrow of a theory of space. Euclidean geometry was the paradigm of certainty attained through *a priori* reasoning, and, more than that, the paradigm held up to the moral philosopher by Plato as well as by Spinoza. Understanding the role played by the ideal of certainty in our intellectual and moral life for over two thousand years and considering carefully the implications of its demise for moral (and social and religious) argument as well as for pure science is not incompatible with appreciating Relativity 'for its own sake' – in fact it is inseparable from doing this properly. And much of the emptiness of current social science arises from the attempt to study social and psychological questions with an entirely false ideal of 'objectivity' which misses even the connections of the social sciences with each other, in addition to missing the questions of the greatest importance to moral reflection.

One caution is in order, however. Dropping false ideals of 'objectivity' does not mean viewing all social science from the standpoint of getting the world out of the mess it is in during, say, the next hundred years. Important as that is, it still falls far short of the ultimate question, which is not how to make individual reforms – even reforms as big as 'socialism' – but *where* do we want to go?

Let me try to summarize these somewhat ranging reflections. I have not tried to demonstrate in this paper that emotive theories of ethical discourse are wrong or that ethical relativism is wrong. That is a subject for technical philosophical papers. I have indicated that, in my opinion, these fashionable and by now widely disseminated philosophical views are wrong, and that some ethical principles at least are likely to have a large measure of objectivity. I have suggested, following the lead of Judy Baker and Paul Grice, that the 'objectivity' of ethical principles, or, more broadly, of 'moralities', is connected with such things as width of appeal, ability to withstand certain kinds of rational criticism (which I have not tried to spell out), feasibility, ideality, and, of course, with how it actually *feels* to live by them or attempt to live by them. I have also pointed out that moral knowledge is what philosophers call 'practical knowledge' as opposed to theoretical knowledge, and that imagination and sensibility are essential *instruments* of practical reasoning. My purpose has not been to defend these views here, but to see what difference these views make, if they are right, not for philosophy but for literature and science.

I have contended that the idea that morality is just 'subjective' and the corollary idea that moral reasoning is either just instrumental (concerned with the selection of means to *arbitrarily* selected ends) or else a contradiction in terms, is terribly destructive not just for morality itself but for all of culture. We can only understand the way in which the literary imagination does really help us to understand ourselves and life, on the one hand, and the way in which science does really bear on metaphysical problems on the other, if we have an adequate view of moral reasoning, where, by moral reasoning, I mean not just reasoning about duty or virtue, but moral reasoning in the widest sense – reasoning about how to live.

* Reprinted, with the kind permission of the editor, from *New Literary*, vol. VII, 1975–6.

PART THREE

REFERENCE
AND UNDERSTANDING

REFERENCE
AND UNDERSTANDING

My thesis is that the theory of language understanding and the theory of reference and truth have much less to do with one another than many philosophers have assumed. I want to explain why this is so. I believe that if I am right, this will shed light on a number of things in philosophy – for example, why Wittgenstein had both a picture theory of meaning and a 'use' theory of meaning (at different times, of course!), and what was going on in nineteenth-century objections to a correspondence theory of truth.

UNDERSTANDING LANGUAGE

It seems to me that the account according to which understanding a language *consists* in being able to use it (or to translate it into a language one *can* use) is the only account now in the field. Perhaps Michael Dummett will succeed in developing an alternative account (I know he wants to); but at present I know of no alternative. Second, I don't think 'ability to use' a language has to be thought of as coming from the learning of separate little playlets of the kind Wittgenstein uses in the early pages of the *Investigations* to illustrate the notion of a 'language game'. Some Wittgensteinians appear to think of language in this way – as consisting of *disconnected* 'uses' (e.g. the expression 'that's a different language game' such persons sometimes use), but I don't think Wittgenstein is guilty of this; and, in any case, it is not essential to the doctrine.

While a *true-to-life* model of the global use of a language is hardly to be hoped for, an *over-simplified* model (for assertorial language) is contained in the work of Carnap and Reichenbach. This is the model of the speaker/hearer as possessing an inductive logic (e.g. a subjective probability metric – although I don't think this is a very good way to view induction), a deductive logic, a preference ordering (although I don't think this is more than an idealized way of modelling human preference structures), and a rule of action (e.g. 'maximize the estimated utility' – although I think this is a bad rule in many situations). Imagine a community of such speaker/hearers who accept sentences they hear others utter (or assign them a high probability) and who are permitted to utter sentences themselves whose probability exceeds a certain value. In even such a terribly over-simplified model, speech will affect behaviour in a rich variety of ways. And the better the inductive logic, the better the deductive logic, the more realistic the utility function, the more the behaviour of these creatures will resemble 'understanding a language'.

Such a model is not tied to an individualistic conception of knowledge or language. Since speakers may acquire knowledge from each other (knowledge is a 'contagious disease', in John McDowell's happy phrase) it is not necessary that each speaker who has a word, say, 'gold', in his vocabulary should be himself able to tell whether or not something is gold. Indeed, as long as each speaker who has the word 'gold' in his vocabulary possesses a *standard minimum amount of information* about gold, he or she will be able to participate in collective discussions about gold. Thus, the feature that I called 'the linguistic division of labour' (in 'The Meaning of "Meaning"'[1]) is perfectly compatible with such a model. Also, another idea I put forward in 'The Meaning of "Meaning"' – the importance of 'stereotypes', conceived of as minimum amounts of information associated with words – is readily assimilated into such a model. Finally, such a model of a speaker/hearer is essentially *holistic* – the conditions under which any particular sentence will be uttered and the behaviour that will result if any given sentence is uttered does not depend upon any isolated thing that could be called the 'sense' of the sentence, but on the total system. Changing the inductive logic, or the deductive logic, or the utility function will to some extent affect the utterance conditions for and the behaviour responses to every sentence of the language (although ordinary statements about macro-observables will, of course, have canonical 'verifying' and 'falsifying' experiences associated with them). However, not every change in 'use' (in the sense of the system, or in the sense of utterance conditions for sentences/behaviour responses to sentences) is a change in *meaning*. Meaning, in my view, is a coarse grid laid over use. I think there are different criteria for saying that there has been a change of meaning in the case of different sorts of words; and for some words (e.g. logical words) there is no sense to the change of meaning/change of theory dichotomy at all. (That our criteria for 'change of meaning' are as various and sloppy as they are is explained by the different kinds of interests we have in connection with different topics and activities. In this sense, language *is* a 'motley' – even if one can bring the motley under a uniform representation at some level of abstraction.)

This is only a sketch of a 'use' account of understanding, but I take it that this sort of account is pretty familiar (except, perhaps, for the idea of meaning as a coarse grid over use). What I want to shift to now are the topics of realism, reference, and truth.

REALISM AND CORRESPONDENCE

Nothing in this account of 'use' says *anything* about a correspondence between words and things, or sentences and states of affairs. But it doesn't follow that such a correspondence doesn't exist. A number of tools have this feature: that the instructions for use of the tool do not mention something that *explains* the successful use of the tool. For example, the instructions for turning an electric light on and off – 'just flip the switch' – do not mention *electricity*. But the explanation of the success of switch-flipping as a method for getting lights to go on and off certainly does mention electricity. It is in this sense that reference and truth have less to do with understanding language than philosophers have tended to assume, in my opinion.

On the model just sketched, one can use one's language, at least on an 'object language' level, without any sophisticated notion of truth. Of course, one has to be able to assent and dissent; but that one has in the Carnap/Reichenbach model. The instructions the mind follows, in this model, do not presuppose notions of the order of 'true'; they are instructions for assigning high weights to certain sentences when one has certain experiences, instructions for uttering, instructions for carrying out syntactic transformations, instructions for producing non-verbal behaviour (e.g. 'lift arm when "lifting arm has maximum estimated utility" is computed'), etc. But the *success* of the 'language-using program' may well depend on the existence of a suitable correspondence between the words of a language and things, and between the sentences of the language and states of affairs. The notions of truth and reference may be of great importance in explaining the relation of language to the world without being as central to meaning theory (in the sense of understanding-of-language theory) as they are in, for example, theories that *equate* understanding with knowledge of truth conditions.

It was this that I had in mind when I spoke of Wittgenstein's two theories of meaning: the picture theory *was* wrong as a theory of understanding, for reasons that Wittgenstein himself very well brought out; but not totally wrong as a theory of language functioning. It *is* essential to view our theories as a kind of 'map' of the world, realists contend, if we are to explain how they help us to guide our conduct as they do. But the 'use' theory is *also* right as an account of how language is *understood*. And the insights are not incompatible: a map, after all, is only a map by virtue of being *employed* in certain ways, but that insight does not contradict but supplements the fact that a map is only successful if it corresponds in an appropriate way to a particular part of the earth, or whatever. Talk of use and talk of reference are parts of the total story, just as talk of switch-flipping and talk of electricity flowing through wires are parts of a total story.

SUCCESS

I have been employing the notion of 'success'. Let me try to unpack this notion. What 'succeeds' or 'fails' is not, in general, linguistic behaviour by itself but total behaviour. E.g. we say certain things, conduct certain reasonings with each other, manipulate materials in a certain way, and finally we have a bridge that enables us to cross a river that we couldn't cross before. And our reasoning and discussion is as much a part of the total organized behaviour-complex as is our lifting of steel girders with a crane. So what I should really speak of is not the success or failure of our linguistic behaviour, but rather the *contribution* of our linguistic behaviour to the success of our total behaviour.

Up to a point, every metaphysical position gives the same explanation of this – of the contribution of linguistic behaviour to the success of total behaviour – but only up to a point. The explanation is that certain kinds of beliefs we hold tend to be *true* (or whatever predicate the position in question substitutes for 'true', e.g. 'warrantedly assertible'). Some philosophers have been so incautious as to put forward the maxim that 'most of a speaker's beliefs are true' as a kind of *a priori* principle governing radical translation; but this seems to me to go too far. (First of all, I don't know how to *count* beliefs. So I don't know what it means to speak of most of a speaker's beliefs. And second, most people's beliefs on *some* topics – e.g. philosophy – are probably *false*.) But most people do have true beliefs about where they live, what the neighbourhood looks like, how to get from one place to another, etc. And they have many true beliefs about how other people will react in various circumstances, and many true beliefs about how to do and make certain things. And *every* philosophical position yields roughly the following story:

(1) People act (in general) in such a way that their goals will be obtained (as well as possible in the given situation), or in such a way that their expectations will not be frustrated, or, in more concrete terms, so that they will get food, lodging, etc., find friends and companions, etc., get from one place to another successfully, avoid dangers, and so on, *if* their beliefs are true.

(2) Many beliefs (of the kinds I mentioned, and of other relevant kinds) *are* true. (Although some are false – which is part of the explanation of people's *failures*.)

(3) So, as a consequence of (1) and (2), people have a tendency to attain certain kinds of goals.

I think this much is non-controversial. Every account of truth tries to make (1) and (2) correct, and thus to permit us to explain (3) via (1) and (2). For example, a pragmatist or phenomenalist account interprets 'true' so that a true statement corresponds to conditional expectations which will be fulfilled if the action which is the antecedent condition for the conditional expectation is carried out. So (1) is taken care of – if one is acting on *true* beliefs, one's expectations won't be frustrated. And all philosophical positions – idealism, pragmatism, realism, etc. (except extreme scepticism) – hold that most beliefs people have about where they live, etc., are true. So (2) is accepted. So in all positions 'truth' plays the same role in accounting for the contribution that linguistic behaviour makes to the success of total behaviour *up to this point* – that one explains (3) via (1) and (2).

However, these are not all the desiderata that one wishes to impose on an account of truth. For example, I have argued elsewhere[2] that some familiar positivist substitutes for the notion of truth (e.g. 'is simple and leads to true predictions') do not have the property that the conjunction of acceptable theories (theories with the property in question) is acceptable. So acceptability is not preserved by deductive logic.[3] But scientists do regard *logical consequences* of acceptable theories as acceptable. (In the sense that, if the consequence is unacceptable, then one has to go back and revise one's decision that *all* the premises were acceptable.) So an account of this kind – an account that says that what we seek is a kind of acceptability that lacks the property of deductive closure – fails to justify norms of scientific practice. It is precisely because there are further desiderata that an account of truth has to satisfy beyond giving us the minimal account of the contribution of linguistic behaviour to the success of total behaviour (by which I mean (1), (2) ∴ (3)) that one has grounds for rejecting some metaphysical positions on the nature of truth and/or acceptability as inadequate.

Besides giving us the minimal account of the contribution of linguistic behaviour to the success of total behaviour, and giving us the fact that truth (or whatever notion of acceptability one may propose as a replacement for truth if one objects to the notion of truth for some reason) is preserved by (suitable[4]) rules of deductive logic, there is one further desideratum in particular that a satisfactory account of truth ought to fulfil: it ought to *account for the reliability of our learning.* Let me now say something about this desideratum.

REALIST ACCOUNTS OF EPISTEMIC RELIABILITY

The minimal account of the contribution of linguistic behaviour to the success of total behaviour employs the idea that most (or at least many) of our beliefs on certain topics are true. But these beliefs are not a definite stock fixed once and for all. They are constantly changing as a result of learning (using the term in a wide sense to include perception). So what premiss (2) of the minimal account really asserts is that certain sorts of learning are *reliable* – in the sense of leading to a large number of true beliefs. How is this reliability to be explained?

Of course, what sort of 'explanation' one thinks is to be given will depend upon features of one's philosophical position. Contemporary realists often differ from realists of earlier centuries in rejecting the notion of *a priori* truth, or at least in not putting very much 'weight' on the notion. They also – here I again take the risk of generalizing about philosophers who have many disagreements among themselves – tend to be sceptical of the idea of a fixed unchanging 'scientific method'. And if one does not regard the methods of gaining knowledge as given *a priori*, and if one regards these methods as enmeshed in and evolving in history, then one will be unlikely to view any sharp dichotomy between the *method* and the *content* of knowledge as defensible.[5] What our 'methods' are in any domain will depend on what our *beliefs* are concerning the subject matter of that domain and on beliefs in other domains. From such a point of view, the problem of explaining the reliability of learning is not to show *a priori* that our learning methods are reliable, but to show that one can understand that reliability as a fact of nature – that one can explain it, or make progress towards explaining it, as one explains or makes progress towards explaining other facts of nature. The possibility of doing this may be viewed as a kind of 'consistency check' (in an informal sense of 'consistency') on the metaphysical view as a whole.

To see how this program can be carried out, let us take the simple case of visual perception: a normal speaker looks at an object, say a rug, and says 'the rug is green' or 'the rug is not green'. Why is he reliable?

Part of the story is the usual causal account of vision. What this yields, to the extent that it has been carried out (and no one would deny that enormous progress has been made in the understanding of colour vision), is an explanation of the following facts:

(4) If the rug is green, then the speaker probably accepts 'the rug is green'.

(5) If the rug is not green, then the speaker probably accepts 'the rug is not green'.

But what we want is:

(6) The speaker probably accepts whichever statement is *true*.

Now the realist also accepts some standard truth definition[6] for the language. Such a truth definition sets up a correspondence between things and words (e.g. *'the rug' refers to some contextually definite rug; 'is green' refers to green things: sentences of the form 'The NV's' are true if and only if the object referred to by 'The N' is referred to by 'V'*.) Such a definition has the features that

(a) It satisfies Tarski's Criterion T, e.g.
'The rug is green' is true if and only if the rug is green,

And

(b) 'True' commutes with truth functions and with such operators as 'probably'.

By virtue of these features, (4) and (5) imply:

(4') If the rug is green, the speaker probably accepts the statement which is true from the pair 'the rug is green', 'the rug is not green'.

(5') If the rug is not green, the speaker probably accepts the statement (from the same pair) which is true.

And since the rug (in the situation envisaged) is either green or not green:

(6') The speaker probably accepts the statement which is true (from the pair in question in the situation envisaged).

Statement (6′) says that a certain form of learning (visual perception in the case of a uniformly coloured rug) is reliable. And we have sketched how a realist can account for this reliability from *within* our total conceptual system (causal theory of perception and language use plus semantic theory of truth), as he reconstructs that conceptual system. Thus the 'consistency check' is satisfactory. (Of course all this is programmatic, but so is our explanation of most empirical facts.) In the case of more complicated kinds of learning, the causal account of reliability is, of course, much more programmatic. But, unless we want to jettison or ignore our entire body of natural science and scientific speculation, no alternative account is even in the field today.

One interesting case is that of inference to a *theory*. Here, as many people have remarked, it seems necessary to assume that we have 'weak *a priori* knowledge' in the sense of having evolved with a 'simplicity ordering' of theories, or a 'prior probability metric', which is not 'too bad' in the sense of not assigning a hopelessly low probability to the theories which are true in the actual world. How this happened we cannot explain; but that it should have happened is at least not *inconsistent* with our present accounts of the development of the species, and much more work is certainly going to be done both on the history of that development and on the structure of our inferential capacities. The messiness of the situation is not a source of dismay to an anti-a prioristic and scientifically minded realist; it is just what he would expect at the present stage of research into a complex problem that cuts across the fields of biology, psychology, and inductive logic!

The role played in this by the idea of a *correspondence* between language items and extra-linguistic reality is not hard to see. The causal theory of reliability tells us that, for example, when a certain state of affairs obtains (the rug being green) the speaker utters a certain sentence ('the rug is green'). The semantic theory of truth tells us that the sentence is *true* just in case that state of affairs obtains – the correspondence involved in the causal story is exactly the correspondence set up by the truth definition. So we can be viewed as systems that reliably produce true sentences when a certain variety of states of affairs obtain. Assumption (2) of the minimal account of the contribution of linguistic behaviour to the success of total behaviour is (sketchily, programmatically) *explained*.

Another desideratum on any account of *truth* is that the correctness of assumption (1) be explained (in the same sense). For most *idealists* this is not a problem – a 'true' statement *is* one that corresponds to the right sort of expectations about the consequences of behaviour. But the idealist has his problems too. If he is not a holist – if statements correspond *one by one* to sets of expectations – then he has trouble explaining the actual character of the development of theories, which is decidedly 'holistic'. If, on the other hand, he makes *truth* (or acceptability) a predicate of large systems of statements – perhaps whole bodies of knowledge – and not single sentences, then he has trouble accounting for the reliability of learning (indeed, I would argue he *can't* explain it – but that goes beyond the present paper).

For the realist, however, (1) is not trivial. 'Snow is white' doesn't correspond to a fixed set of expectations about the future, on his account, but to snow being white. So how does it come about that when we believe certain statements we tend to act in a way which will not frustrate our expectations *if* those statements are true (i.e. if the corresponding states of affairs obtain)?

The realist's answer is that the *connection* between the state of affairs in question obtaining and our goal's being satisfied is *itself* something about which we have many true beliefs. We have true beliefs of the form 'If I do X, then I will get Y'. How does this come about? Well, these connections are themselves *learned* – thus the (programmatic) causal account of the reliability of learning *also* explains the existence of true beliefs about *connections* between actions and goals in various situations.

It is this causal account of the correctness of both assumptions of the minimal account of the contribution of linguistic behaviour to the success of total behaviour that I had in mind when I said at the beginning that the *correspondence* between words and things, between statements and states of affairs, is what explains the success of language using even if it isn't referred to in the 'program' for language using.

So far I have left it seeming miraculous that the relation between states of affairs and sentences described by the causal theory of perception, language acquisition etc., is *also* the one specified by a truth definition for the language. But this too can be accounted for. Let C be an arbitrary correspondence between sentences and states of affairs, and call a sentence TRUE (C) if the state of affairs to which it bears the relation C obtains. Then there is in general no reason why the property of being TRUE (C) should be preserved by deductive logic. But it is part of our explanation of speakers' reliability that one of the ways in which they acquire new beliefs is the use of deductive logic and that deductive logic preserves *truth*.[7] If this explanation is to be a part of the total explanation of reliability, then the correspondence C has to be of a special kind and the most natural choice is a correspondence which is based on a satisfaction relation.

Once we pick a correspondence of this kind to define *truth-in-L*, where L is the language in question, it will, of course, be possible to define the correspondence in question in any meta-language of sufficient strength that contains L itself 'disquotationally' – that is, so that the Criterion T is satisfied. Note that (T) has no significance in radical translation, however[8] – and I argue in my John Locke Lectures that the truth-definition for a natural language is under-determined by the sort of causal considerations discussed here, and that there may well be some interest-relativity to notions like 'truth' and 'reference' in the context of radical translation. The fact that explanations may be interest-relative doesn't mean that they can't be *correct*, however – which is all that is needed for the argument I am advancing for realism.

IS THE CAUSAL EXPLANATION PHILOSOPHICALLY NEUTRAL?

I can imagine a philosopher responding to what I have just said by saying, 'Of course, what you have sketched is the *scientific* explanation of the reliability of learning' – the thrust being that such a *scientific* explanation must be compatible with *any* meta-physical position. Now, of course all metaphysical positions claim to be compatible with all of science, but claiming it doesn't make it so.

In order to see what the difficulties are that face the nonrealist philosopher who wishes to incorporate the causal explanation of the success of language using into his world picture, I shall discuss one position in particular. This is the position I described in 'What is "Realism"?'[9] (a position suggested by some ideas of Michael Dummett). In "What is Realism"? I showed that by giving a quasi-intuitionist meaning to the logical connectives we could preserve all of extensional scientific discourse, and also preserve Tarskian semantics (including Criterion T), while avoiding any commitment to the existence of theoretical entities such as genes or molecules. So, at first blush it seems that one could take over the entire causal explanation of the contribution of linguistic behaviour to the success of total behaviour, without really being committed to the existence of most of the entities science talks about, or the existence of a correspondence between words and such entities. Causal realism *within* science would appear to be compatible with an idealist reinterpretation of total science.

But, I went on to argue, this is not so. For science as ordinarily understood makes *modal* statements – statements about what is and is not *possible* – e.g. 'one can't build a perpetual motion machine'. And a reinterpretation of science that is not to be a mutilation must also 'translate' these statements (preserving truth-value, and preserving inductive and deductive relations). But this, I claim, one cannot do.

To see why not, I first point out that 'truth', on the quasi-intuitionist picture, becomes a version of warranted assertibility. (It is, of course, quite typical of idealist reconstructions that the predicates offered as notions of acceptability to replace the classical notion of truth are versions of warranted assertibility.)

Now, in the case of seeing what colour a rug is, it is a part of the causal explanation that there is *room for error* – it is *physically* possible that one seems to see a green rug, etc., and the rug *not* be green. Thus:

(7) 'The rug is green' might be warrantedly assertible even though the rug is not green.

is a modal statement implied by our theory. But this shows truth *can't* be warranted assertibility!

My argument has been described by Dummett as a sort of 'naturalistic fallacy' argument (one might call it the 'idealistic fallacy argument'), because of its obvious similarity to Moore's celebrated argument for the indefinability of 'good'. What I am claiming is that for any predicate P the idealist may want to substitute for 'true' one can find a statement S such that

(8) S might have property P and still not be *true*.

follows from our causal theory of learning. And this is so simply because the 'slop' between being warrantedly assertible, no matter how construed, and being *true* (assuming only Criterion T) is itself 'built in' to our causal theory.

It might seem, however, that Dummett has an easy way out. Suppose might-statements are confirmed by the realist by describing a 'model' in which the statement in question holds (satisfying the specified constraints) and showing that the model satisfies the *laws* of our theory. Very well, let the non-realist accept this as the verification-procedure (warranted assertibility procedure) for might-statements, and adjoin them to *his* language with this same verification procedure.

Then with 'true' (warrantedly assertible) extended to statements of the form 'p might be true even if q' in this way, it will also hold for the non-realist that (7) is true, and hence that

(9) 'The rug is green' might be warrantedly assertible even though 'The rug is green' is not true.

What has gone wrong is not hard to show. 'Truth' was reinterpreted as warranted assertibility (in a certain sense). And *asserting that p* was reinterpreted as asserting that *p is warrantedly assertible*. 'The rug is green' is now *entailed by* 'The rug is green is warrantedly assertible'. So if we introduce might-statements into the language as just suggested, we will be giving up the *incompatibility* between *p entails q* and *p might be even if not q*. We should not have preserved the deductive relations between statements in the translation process.

Actually, the problem is even worse: if the new entailments are allowed to be used in the scientific theory itself, it becomes inconsistent. Also, 'true' fails to commute with 'might': 'p might be even if q' fails to be equivalent to 'p might be true even if q is true'.

I have discussed Dummett's position because it represents the most viable nonrealist position I know of. The difficulties it faces reveal how hard it is to provide an idealist reinterpretation of our causal theories that preserves deductive and inductive relations between our statements, including the *modal* statements we accept, and at the same time avoids my idealistic fallacy argument.

THE NINETEENTH CENTURY REVISITED

The great nineteenth-century argument against the correspondence theory of truth was that one cannot think of truth as correspondence to facts (or 'reality') because, so it was contended, thinking of truth in this way would require one to be able to compare concepts directly with unconceptualized reality – and philosophers were as fond then as they are now of pointing out the absurdity of such a comparison.

Needless to say, many different things were going on in this argument – too many to discuss here. (E.g. part of the background to the argument was the general view that we cannot really perceive material objects – a view that has come under heavy fire in the second half of the twentieth century.) But one thing which may well have been in people's minds is the following argument: assume, as is plausible, that to understand a statement is to be explained as *knowing its truth conditions*. If truth is correspondence to reality, it would seem as if knowledge of *what the correspondence is* is presupposed by knowledge *that* such and such a statement stands in the relation in question to anything or does not stand in the relation in question to anything. And if *understanding the statement* is equated with knowing what it is for it to be the case that it stands or does not stand in the relation in question to appropriate entities, then knowledge of what the correspondence is is presupposed in the understanding of *every* statement. But in what could this knowledge – which does not consist in the acceptance of any *statements*, because it is prior to the understanding of all statements – consist?

The semantic theory underlying this form of the objection – the theory that *truth* is prior to *meaning* (i.e. that truth must be the central concept in a theory of understanding[10]) is familiar enough in the present day. What I am suggesting in this paper is that we reject this view. If we view language understanding as the possession of a rational activity of language use – an activity involving 'language entry rules' (procedures for subjecting some sentences to stimulus control[11]), procedures for deductive and inductive inference, and 'language exit rules' (procedures for, e.g. 'taking something in one's hand when one decides it would be optimal to take this in one's hand') – then implicit knowledge of truth conditions is not *presupposed* in any way by the understanding of the language. To put the point more briefly: one does not need to *know* that there is a correspondence between words and extra-linguistic entities to learn one's language. But there is such a correspondence none the less, and it explains the *success* of what one is doing. *After* one has learned one's language one can talk about *anything* – including the correspondence in question. Wittgenstein's view in the *Tractatus* that the correspondence in question cannot be described but only 'shown' is true in only a limited sense: even if one follows Kripke rather than Tarski so that the relation of reference can be spoken of in the object language itself rather than only in a meta-language, a wider relation of reference can still be defined by going up a level of language.

But still, even this wider relation of reference can still be spoken about and not merely 'shown'. And for the purposes of the kind of causal explanation of the reliability of learning, etc., discussed above the relation of reference that we can speak of in the object language itself is perfectly sufficient. As Carnap long ago emphasized, there is nothing 'indescribable' in the relation of language to the world.

A REALIST OBJECTION

I can imagine that some realists may well be uncomfortable with the account of understanding sketched here, even as an idealized and terribly over-simplified model. Isn't this model a verificationist one? And isn't verificationism at bottom a form of idealism?

To take the first charge first: I *am* saying that there was an important insight hidden in verificationism. The insight is that in any plausible model of a speaker/hearer the assignment of a 'probability' or some not-necessarily-quantitative analogue of 'probability' to sentences (though not necessarily to *every* sentence, on observational evidence – language is also used to discuss what *would* happen under circumstances that we might not be able to confirm if they existed, e.g. phenomena in the interior of black holes) is going to play a central role. In *Experience and Prediction*, Reichenbach illustrates the power of what he calls the 'probability theory of meaning' in the following way: a traditional phenomenalist has to explain talk about unobserved objects – say, unobserved trees – by 'reducing' it to talk about observed objects (and ultimately to sense-impressions) in the fashion of Mach or Avenarius. But Reichenbach does not have to do this. A sentence about unobserved trees (e.g. 'there is a tree behind me') is understood if we know how to assign it a 'weight' – i.e. how to conclude to it inductively (Reichenbach leaves out the need for a utility function and a decision rule – these come in in Carnap's later work on probability), how to deduce/induce consequences from it, etc. For example, suppose I see a tree shadow (as if of a tree behind my left shoulder). Previously I have confirmed: 'whenever there is a tree shadow, there is a tree in such and such a spatial relation to the tree shadow'. From this inductively confirmed generalization and the observation of the tree shadow in front of me I deduce (or induce, if the generalization is itself only statistical), 'there is a tree in such and such a spatial relation to *this* tree shadow', and, finally, 'there is a tree behind me'. So I have now accepted (or assigned a weight to) a sentence about an unobserved tree without any Machian (or C. I. Lewisian, or Russellian, etc.) 'reduction' of the unobserved tree to a series of actual or possible observed trees or sense impressions. (A similar account is given by Carnap in *Testability and Meaning*.)

What seems right to me about this is that if we had no inductive logic *at all* – if we only had pattern recognition and deductive logic – there would be no basis for ascribing to us any *concept* of an 'unobserved object'. Our linguistic behaviour would fit the account '"tree" means "observed tree"' – and, more generally, '"object" means "observed object"'. In this sense, our inductive logic is *part of* our concept of an unobserved object, and hence of an object at all. (Which doesn't mean that every *change* in our inductive logic is a change in our concept of an object – notions like 'concept' and 'meaning' are a coarse grid over use.) Similarly, our deductive logic is part of our understanding of what a set or property is, as well as of our understanding of the quantifiers and connectives.

Second, it is *not* clear that *this* form of verificationism (the 'probability theory of meaning') is incompatible with realism. (I think the 'probability theory of meaning' is *wrong* on quite different grounds, but that is not the question here. The question I want to look at for a moment is whether the 'probability theory of meaning' is compatible with realism or not.)

It is clear why the 'conclusive verifiability in principle' theory of meaning is incompatible with realism. The realist believes that the truth or falsity of our sentences depends (usually) on something *external* – i.e. on facts which are not (logically equivalent to) experiential facts, facts which are not about sensations (or about language rules, etc.). But realism, if true, must be expressible in some language or other. ('If you can't say it you can't whistle it either.') Suppose LR is a language adequate for the expression of the thesis of realism. E.g. in LR we might want to give the sort of account I have been sketching, of how there is a correspondence between sentences and extra-linguistic (and nonphenomenal) facts the existence of which explains the contribution language using makes to the success of over-all behaviour. If conclusive verificationism is correct, there must be phenomenal truth conditions for every sentence in every intelligible language. (Or else conditions in 'observable thing language', if the dispute is about realism with respect to 'theoretical entities' rather than with respect to non-phenomenal entities. But I shall ignore this refinement.) So, in particular, the sentences of LR which purport to describe the allegedly non-phenomenal states of affairs corresponding to the sentences of, say, natural language, actually have phenomenal truth conditions – i.e. these states of affairs are not really non-phenomenal after all. So realism is either false or (worse) inexpressible.

But no such argument can be offered against the compatibility of realism with the 'probability theory of meaning'. Why should it be impossible from a realist point of view that (1) every meaningful sentence have some weight or other in some observable situation, and (2) every *difference* in meaning be reflected in some difference in weight in some observable situation? (These are, in my formulation, the two principles of Reichenbach's 'probability theory of meaning'.) At least it should be an open question for the realist *qua* realist whether this is so or not, and not something that realism rules out.

However, it is very important in this connection that the 'probability theory of meaning' does not require that every meaningful sentence have a *high* weight (be 'verified') in some situation or other. For this would rule out such sentences as 'there is a gold mountain but "there is a gold mountain" will never have a high weight on the evidence'. And to insist on a *semantical* connection between existence and knowledge is unacceptable to a realist. Similarly, to require that every meaningful sentence be 'falsifiable in principle' (have a low 'weight' in some observable situation) would be unacceptable to a realist. But neither Carnap nor Reichenbach imposes these requirements.

However, it *is* unacceptable to a realist simply to take the 'probability theory of meaning' as an *explication* of meaningfulness, as Reichenbach does. Let S_1 and S_2 be sentences describing two states of affairs which are possible according to physical theory and not equivalent according to the laws of the physical theory. Before a realist could accept the 'probability theory of meaning', *one* thing he would have to be shown is that every such pair S_1, S_2 has the property that in some observable situation or other S_1 and S_2 differ in weight. (If we allow differences in weight on *non*-observational evidence to count as differences in meaning, then this problem may disappear, but then the theory is not verificationist any more.) The realist would not be willing to simply stipulate that S_1 and S_2 *count* as the same situation just *because* they get the same weight on all observational evidence.[12]

Moreover, the 'probability theory of meaning' seems wrong to me as an account of *meaning* anyhow. It cannot as it stands incorporate either the linguistic division of labour (the fact that confirmation procedures for *being gold* or *being aluminum*, or *being an elm tree*, or *being David* are not the property of every speaker – the speakers defer to experts for the fixing of reference in a huge number of cases) or the contribution of the environment (the fact that the extension of a term sometimes fixes its meaning and not vice versa[13]). In my view, the criteria used by experts to tell whether or not something is gold are not 'part of the meaning' of *gold* (i.e. the word doesn't change its meaning in the language if the experts shift to a different set of tests for the same metal), yet they are part of a mechanism for fixing the extension of *gold*. But if they are not part of the *meaning* of *gold*, then there is nothing in the meaning to enable us *individually* to assign a 'weight' to 'such and such is gold' – contrary to the 'probability theory of meaning'.

But I did not argue that we should accept the 'probability theory of meaning'. I only argued that the Reichenbach–Carnap model is partly correct as an account of *use* and *understanding*, not as an account of *meaning*.

USE AND MEANING

If the account I have offered here is correct, it is clear why we want a notion of reference; but what is the need for a notion of meaning?

We need a notion of reference because the referent of a term is important in many different situations. Buying and selling wine is quite a different 'language game' from discussing wine at the dinner table; but the extension of the term 'wine' may be the same in both contexts, and the truth conditions for 'one can buy Israeli wine in this country' may be the same in both contexts. And it is *because* a sentence can have the same truth conditions in different contexts that the same inductive and deductive logic can be used in different contexts. But again, what is the need for a notion of meaning?

In my view,[14] a language made up and used by a being who belonged to no community would have no need for such a concept as the *meaning* of a term. To state the reference of each (simple and defined) term and to describe what the language user believes in connection with each term is to tell the whole story. If the language changes so that the reference of any term changes, we can say that this has happened; or if the speaker revises some of his beliefs we can say that this has happened; but why say that some (but not all) of the latter changes count as 'changes of meaning'?

But as soon as the language becomes a communal instrument things change. How could *discussion* take place if we could assume *nothing* about what all speakers believe? Could I safely use the word 'tiger' in talking to you if, for all I knew, you believed that tigers are a kind of *clam*? Where would conversation start?

In 'The Meaning of "Meaning"', I argued that meaning is a several-component affair. I put forward the view that *one* component of meaning is the *reference* (extension). (In my view, reference is fixed by meaning only in the sense of being a *component of* meaning, but not in the sense that meaning is a mechanism for fixing reference. The actual mechanisms for fixing reference – e.g. the criteria used by experts to tell whether or not something is gold – are *not* always part of meaning.) Another major component, in my view, is *stereotype* – and stereotypes are nothing but standardized sets of beliefs or idealized beliefs associated with terms. (E.g. the belief that tigers are typically striped orange and black is part of our stereotype of a tiger.) The need for stereotypes is *not* primarily to fix extensions; that can be and often is done by experts using criteria that are not 'part of the meaning' in any sense. The stereotype associated with 'gold', for example, is all but worthless for fixing the extension of the word (or its extension in possible worlds, for that matter). *Language is not only used to verify and falsify and classify*; it is also used to *discuss*. The existence of standardized stereotypes, and hence of meaning, is a necessity for *discussion*, not for classification.

Incidentally, Wittgenstein was right in saying that language is a motley, *in the sense that* we have many different standards for different types of discussion – and this reflects itself in the fact that the *amount* of information contained in 'meanings', the *nature* of the information, and its logical 'tightness' (approximation to analyticity), varies enormously from kind of word to kind of word, and even between words of one kind. (Compare 'bachelor' and 'gold', and also 'gold' and 'molybdenum'. 'Gold' and 'molybdenum' are both names of metals – but there is a rich stereotype of gold and virtually no stereotype of molybdenum beyond the feature 'metal'. Again, 'tiger' and 'weasel' are both names of animals – but the stereotype (and, in my view, the meaning) of 'tiger' includes the feature of having orange and black stripes whereas I have no idea what colour weasels are, and *a fortiori* no idea by virtue of 'knowing the meaning' of 'weasel'.)

MORALS

If there are any morals to be drawn from my discussion, they are perhaps (1) that the notion that one learns one's native language by learning *what the truth conditions are* for its various sentences has no presently intelligible sense, at least for a realist; (2) that it does not follow that the realist's notions of truth and reference are not important for the discussion of language – but their importance is for the explanation of the contribution linguistic behaviour makes to the success of total behaviour, not to a theory of understanding; and (3) since (as I have argued elsewhere) the notion of 'meaning' has neither the nature nor the function philosophers believe it to have, the injection of the word 'meaning' into discussions of understanding and use is more likely to confuse than to clarify issues.

NOTES

1 Cf. My *Mind, Language, and Reality; Philosophical Papers,* vol. 2, Cambridge University Press, 1975, ch. 12.

2 In *ibid.,* ch. 11.

3 However, a certain kind of 'warranted assertibility' *is* preserved by a *non-classical* logic. The possibility of replacing the realist notion of truth with a notion of warranted assertibility by interpreting the logic of natural language as nonclassical was suggested by Michael Dummett (this is more or less hinted at in his famous paper on Truth ('Truth', *Proceedings of the Aristotelian Society,* vol. 59 (1958–9), pp. 141–62) and is discussed by me in 'What is "Realism"?' (*Proceedings of the Aristotelian Society* (1975–6), pp. 177–94).

4 I believe that it is possible to decide that classical logic is incorrect for realist rather than intuitionist reasons (cf. note 7, below). But in this case the theorist must show that the correct logic (according to the new theory) has classical logic as a 'special case' in many situations, so that the appropriateness of using classical logic *where it is successful* can be accounted for.

5 An interesting defence of this version of realism is Richard Boyd's 'A Causal Theory of Evidence', *Nous,* vol. 7 (1973), pp. 1–12.

6 I use the term 'truth definition' in the sense of standard Tarskian semantics. An interesting variant has recently been proposed by Saul Kripke in 'Outline of a Theory of Truth', *Journal of Philosophy,* vol. LXXII, no. 19 (6 November 1975), pp. 690–715. This variant permits *reference* and *truth* to be talked of *in the object language itself* at the cost of modifying Tarski's Criterion T.

7 If my position on quantum mechanics is correct (in *Mathematics, Matter, and Method; Philosophical Papers,* vol. 1, Cambridge University Press, 1975, ch. 10) and the actual logic of the world is not classical logic but the modular logic described by Birkhoff and von Neumann, or something similar, then we would have to say: 'classical deductive logic preserves

truth in situations in which quantum mechanics can be ignored', instead of what is in the text.

8 I discuss this and also the interest-relativity of truth-definitions in radical translation in my John Locke Lectures (see Part I).

9 'What is "Realism"?' *Proceedings of the Aristotelian Society* (1975–6), pp. 177–94.

10 Here I employ the terminology of Michael Dummett's (unpublished) William James Lectures. Although our positions clash, I have been enormously stimulated by Dummett's important work, and this paper is largely a response.

11 Again, the idea of 'stimulus control' is only an over-simplification or idealization. Acceptance of an observation sentence by the human mind certainly depends upon attention and global theory in complex ways, not just built in or learned routines of pattern recognition.

12 The presence of a kind of Gödelian incompleteness in any formalized *inductive* logic is also a great difficulty for the 'probability theory of meaning'. Which of the possible formalized inductive logics are we to use in computing 'weight'? (The Gödelian incompleteness of inductive logics was first pointed out in my *Mathematics, Matter, and Method; Philosophical Papers*, vol. 1, Cambridge University Press, 1975, ch. 17, and is also discussed in chapter 18 of the same book.)

13 Cf. 'The Meaning of "Meaning"'.

14 For a detailed statement, see 'The Meaning of "Meaning"'.

PART FOUR

REALISM AND REASON

REALISM AND REASON

In one way of conceiving it, realism is an empirical theory.[1] One of the facts that this theory explains is the fact that scientific theories tend to 'converge' in the sense that earlier theories are, very often, limiting cases of later theories (which is why it is possible to regard theoretical terms as preserving their reference across most changes of theory). Another of the facts it explains is the more mundane fact that language-using contributes to getting our goals, achieving satisfaction, or what have you.

The realist explanation, in a nutshell, is not that language mirrors the world but that *speakers* mirror the world – i.e. their environment – in the sense of *constructing a symbolic representation of that environment*. In 'Reference and Understanding'[2] I argued that a 'correspondence' between words and sets of things (formally, a *satisfaction relation*, in the sense of Tarski) can be viewed as part of an *explanatory model* of the speakers' collective behaviour.

I'm not going to review this in this Address; but let me refer to realism in this sense – acceptance of this sort of scientific picture of the relation of speakers to their environment, and of the role of language – as *internal* realism.

Metaphysical realism, on the other hand, is less an empirical theory than a model – in the 'colliding billiard balls' sense of 'model'. It is, or purports to be, a model of the relation of *any* correct theory to all or part of THE WORLD. I have come to the

Presidential Address to the Eastern Division of the American Philosophical Association, Boston, Mass., 29 December 1976.

conclusion that this model is incoherent. This is what I want to share with you.

Let us set out the model in its basic form.

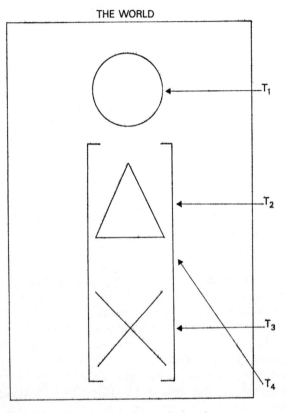

In its primitive form, there is a relation between each term in the language and a piece of THE WORLD (or a *kind* of piece, if the term is a general term).

This relation, the relation of reference, is given *by the truth – conditional semantics* for the language, in the canonical versions of the theory – i.e. *understanding* a term, say, T_1, consists in knowing what piece of THE WORLD it refers to (or in knowing a necessary and sufficient condition for it to refer to a piece of THE WORLD, in some versions). I shall not assume this account of understanding to be part of the picture in what follows, although it certainly was assumed by metaphysical realists in the past.

Minimally, however, there has to *be* a determinate relation of *reference* between terms in L and pieces (or sets of pieces) of THE WORLD, on the metaphysical realist model, whether *understanding* L is taken to consist in 'knowing' that relation or not. What makes this picture different from *internal* realism (which employs a similar picture *within* a theory) is that (1) the picture is supposed to apply to *all* correct theories at once (so that it can only be stated with 'typical ambiguity' – i.e. it transcends complete formalization in any one theory); and (2) THE WORLD is supposed to be *independent* of any particular representation we have of it – indeed, it is held that we might be *unable* to represent THE WORLD correctly at all (e.g. we might all be 'brains in a vat', the metaphysical realist tells us).

The most important consequence of metaphysical realism is that *truth* is supposed to be *radically non-epistemic* – we might be 'brains in a vat' and so the theory that is 'ideal' from the point of view of operational utility, inner beauty and elegance, 'plausibility', simplicity, 'conservatism', etc., *might be false*. 'Verified' (in any operational sense) does not imply 'true', on the metaphysical realist picture, even in the ideal limit.

It is this feature that distinguishes metaphysical realism, as I am using the term, from the mere belief that there *is* an ideal theory (Peircean realism), or, more weakly, that an ideal theory is a regulative ideal presupposed by the notions 'true' and 'objective' as they have classically been understood. And it is this feature that I shall attack!

So let T_1 be an ideal theory, by our lights. Lifting restrictions on our actual all-too-finite powers, we can imagine T_1 to have every property *except objective truth* – which is left open – that we like. E.g. T_1 can be imagined complete, consistent, to predict correctly all observation sentences (as far as we can tell), to meet whatever 'operational constraints' there are (if these are 'fuzzy', let T_1 seem *clearly* to meet them), to be 'beautiful', 'simple', 'plausible', etc. The supposition under consideration is that T_1 might be all this *and still be* (in reality) *false*.

I assume THE WORLD has (or can be broken into) infinitely many pieces. I also assume T_1 *says* there are infinitely many things (so in *this* respect T_1 *is* 'objectively right' about THE WORLD). Now T_1 is *consistent* (by hypothesis) and has (only) infinite models. So by the completeness theorem (in its model theoretic form),

T_1 has a model of every infinite cardinality. Pick a model M of the same cardinality as THE WORLD.[3] Map the individuals of M one-to-one into the pieces of THE WORLD, and use the mapping to define relations of M directly in THE WORLD. The result is a satisfaction relation SAT – a 'correspondence' between the terms of L and sets of pieces of THE WORLD – such that the theory T_1 comes out *true* – true of THE WORLD – provided we just interpret 'true' as TRUE(SAT).[4] So what becomes of the claim that even the *ideal* theory T_1 might *really* be false?

Well, it might be claimed that SAT is not the *intended* correspondence between L and THE WORLD. What does 'intended' come to here?

T_1 has the property of meeting all *operational* constraints. So, if 'there is a cow in front of me at such-and-such a time' belongs to T_1, then 'there is a cow in front of me at such-and-such a time' will certainly *seem* to be true – it will be 'exactly as if' there were a cow in front of me at that time. But SAT is a *true* interpretation of T_1. T_1 is TRUE(SAT). So 'there is a cow in front of me at such-and-such a time' is 'True' in this sense – TRUE(SAT).

On the other hand, if 'there is a cow in front of me at such-and-such a time' is *operationally* 'false' (falsified) then 'there is a cow in front of me at such-and-such a time' is FALSE(SAT). So, the interpretation of 'reference' in L as SAT certainly meets all *operational* constraints on reference. But the interpretation of 'reference' as SAT certainly meets all *theoretical* constraints on reference – it makes the *ideal* theory, T_1, come out *true*.

So what *further* constraints on reference are there that could single out some other interpretation as (uniquely) 'intended', and SAT as an 'unintended' interpretation (in the model-theoretic sense of 'interpretation')? The supposition that even an 'ideal' theory (from a pragmatic point of view) might *really* be false appears to collapse into *unintelligibility*.

Notice that a 'causal' theory of reference is not (would not be) of any help here: for how 'causes' can uniquely refer is as much of a puzzle as how 'cat' can, on the metaphysical realist picture.

The problem, in a way, is traceable back to Occam. Occam introduced the idea that concepts are (mental) *particulars*. If concepts are particulars ('signs'), then any concept we may have of the *relation* between a sign and its object is *another sign*. But it is unintelligible, from my point of view, how the sort of relation the metaphysical realist envisages as holding between a sign and its object can be singled out either by holding up the sign itself, thus

```
COW
```

or by holding up yet another sign, thus

```
REFERS
```

or perhaps

```
CAUSES
```

If concepts are not particulars, on the other hand, the obvious possibility is that (in so far as they are 'in the head') they are *ways of using* signs. But a 'use' theory, while intelligible (and, I believe, correct) as an account of what *understanding* the signs consists in, *does not single out a unique relation* between the terms of T_1 and the 'real objects'. If we don't think concepts are *either* particulars (signs) *or* ways of using signs, then, I think we are going to be led back to direct (and mysterious) grasp of Forms.

Suppose we (and all other sentient beings) are and always were 'brains in a vat'. Then how does it come about that *our* word 'vat' refers to *noumenal* vats and not to vats in the image?

If the foregoing is not to be just a new antinomy, then one has to show that there is at least one intelligible position for which it does *not* arise. And there is. It does not arise for the position Michael Dummett has been defending. Let me explain:

Dummett's idea[5] is to do the *theory of understanding* in terms of the notions of *verification* and *falsification*. This is what he calls 'non-realist semantics'.

What makes this different from the old phenomenalism is that there is no 'basis' of hard facts (e.g. sense data) with respect to which one ultimately uses the truth conditional semantics, classical logic, and the *realist* notions of truth and falsity. The analogy is with mathematical intuitionism: the intuitionist uses *his* notion of 'truth' – constructive provability – *even when talking about constructive proof itself*. Understanding a sentence, in this semantics, is knowing what constitutes a proof (verification) of it. And this is true *even of the sentences that describe verifications*. Thus, I might take 'I have a red sense datum' as a primitive sentence, or I might take 'I see a cow', or, if I do the semantics from the point of view of the brain rather than the person, I might take 'such and such neurons fired'.

Whatever language I use, a primitive sentence – say, 'I see a cow' – will be assertible if and only if *verified*. And we say it is verified *by saying the sentence itself*, 'I see a cow'. To use a term of Roderick Firth's, 'I see a cow' is 'self-warranting' in this kind of epistemology – not in the sense of being *incorrigible*, not even necessarily in the sense of being fully determinate (i.e. obeying strong bivalence – being determinately true or false). (Facts are 'soft all the way down' on this picture, Dummett says.) The important point is that the realist concepts of truth and falsity are not used in this semantics at all.

Now the puzzle about what singles out one correspondence as *the* relation of reference does not arise. The notion of 'reference' is not used in the semantics. We can introduce 'refers' into the language *à la* Tarski, but then

(1) 'Cow' refers to cows

will simply be a tautology – and the *understanding* of (1) makes no reference to the metaphysical realist picture at all.

One important point. It is no good to do the nonrealist semantics (I would rather call it *verificationist semantics* – because it is not incompatible with *internal* realism) in terms of any level of 'hard facts', even sense data. For if sense data are treated as 'hard data' – if the verificationist semantics is given in a meta-language *for* which itself we give the *truth-conditional* account of understanding – then we can repeat the whole argument against the intelligibility of metaphysical realism (as an argument against the intelligibility of the *meta*-language) -- just think of the *past* sense data (or the *future* ones) as the 'external' part of THE WORLD. (This is a reconstruction of one aspect of Wittgenstein's private language argument.) This is why Dummett's move depends upon using the verificationist semantics all the way up (or down) – in the meta-language, the meta-meta-language, etc.

The reason I got involved in this problem is this: in 'Reference and Understanding' I argued that one could give a *model of a speaker* of the language in terms of the notion of 'degree of confirmation' (which might better be called 'degree of verification' when it has this understanding-theoretic role). And I contended that the realist notions of truth and reference come in not in explaining what goes on 'in the heads' of speakers, but in *explaining the success* of language-using. Thus I urged that we accept a species of 'verificationist' semantics. (Though not in the sense of verificationist theory of *meaning* – for, as I have argued elsewhere, [6] 'meaning' is not just a function of what goes on 'in our heads', but also of *reference*, and reference is determined by *social* practices and by actual physical paradigms, and not just by what goes on inside any individual speaker.) But, I claimed, one can still be a *realist* even though one accepts this 'verificationist' model. For the realist claim that there is a correspondence between words and things is not *incompatible* with a 'verificationist' or 'use' account of understanding. Such a correspondence, in my view, is part of an *explanatory theory* of the speakers' interaction with their environment.

The point is that Dummett and I *agree* that you can't treat understanding a sentence (in general) as knowing its truth conditions; because it then becomes unintelligible what *that* knowledge *in turn* consists in. We both *agree* that the theory of understanding has to be done in a verificationist way. (Although I don't think that theory of understanding is all of theory of *meaning* that is of no help *here* – theory of meaning, on my view, presupposes theory of understanding *and reference* – and reference is what the problem is all about!) But now it looks as if in conceding that *some* sort of verificationist semantics must be given as our account of understanding (or 'linguistic competence', in Chomsky's sense), I have given Dummett all he needs to demolish metaphysical realism – a picture I was wedded to!

So what? At this point, *I* think that a natural response would be the following: So metaphysical realism collapses. But internal realism – the empirical theory of 'Reference and Understanding' – doesn't collapse (I claim). Metaphysical realism was only a *picture* anyway. If the picture is, indeed, incoherent, then the moral is surely *not* that something is wrong with realism *per se*, but simply that realism *equals* internal realism. *Internal realism is all the realism we want or need.*

Indeed, I believe that this is true. But it isn't *all* the moral. Metaphysical realism collapsed *at a particular point.* (I am going to argue that it also collapses at other points.) And the point at which it collapsed tells us something. Metaphysical realism collapses just at the point at which it claims to be distinguishable from Peircean realism – i.e. from the claim that there is an ideal theory (I don't mean that even *that* claim isn't problematical, but it is problematical in a different way). Since Peirce himself (and the verificationists) always *said* metaphysical realism collapses into incoherence at *just* that point, and realists like myself thought they were *wrong*, there is no avoiding the unpleasant admission that 'they were right and we were wrong' on at least one substantive issue.

I now want to talk about other points at which the metaphysical realist picture is incoherent. Consider the following simple universe: let 'the world' be a *straight line*, thus

(If you want, there can be one-dimensional people – with apologies to Marcuse – on the line. How you tell the boys from the girls, I don't know.)

Consider the following two stories about THE WORLD:[7]

Story 1. *There are points* – i.e. the line has parts which are line *segments*, and also infinitely small parts called 'points'. The *same relation* – 'part of' – holds between points and line segments which contain them, and between line segments and bigger line segments (and between any piece of the line and the whole line).

Story 2. *There are no points* – the line and its parts all have *extension*. 'Of course,' the teller of this story says, 'I'm not saying Story 1 is *false*. You just have to understand that *points* are logical constructions out of line segments. Point talk is highly derived talk about convergent sets of line segments.'

A 'hard-core' realist might claim that there is a 'fact of the matter' as to which is true – Story 1 or Story 2. But 'sophisticated realists', as I have called them, concede that Story 1 and Story 2 are 'equivalent descriptions'. In effect, this concedes that line segments are a suitable set of 'invariants' – a description of

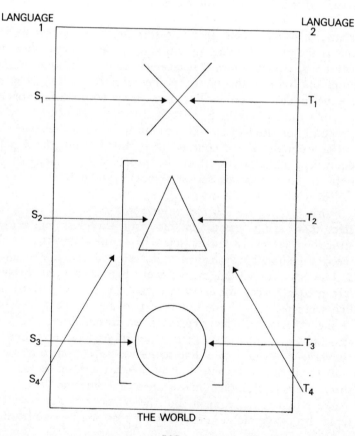

LANGUAGE 1

LANGUAGE 2

S_1 T_1

S_2 T_2

S_3 T_3

S_4 T_4

THE WORLD

THE WORLD which says what is going on in every line segment is a *complete* description. In the past, I argued that this is no problem for the realist – it's just like the fact that the earth can be mapped by different 'projections', I said (Mercator, Polar, etc.). The metaphysical realist picture now looks as on p. 131.

In particular, I believed, it can happen that what we picture as 'incompatible' terms can be mapped onto the same real object – though not, of course, within the same theory. Thus the real object that is labelled 'point' in one theory might be labelled 'set of convergent line segments' in another theory. And the *same* term might be mapped onto one real object in one theory and onto a different real object in another theory. It is a property of the world itself, I claimed – i.e. a property of THE WORLD itself – that it 'admits of these different mappings'.

The problem – as Nelson Goodman has been emphasizing for many, many years – is that this story may retain THE WORLD but at the price of giving up any intelligible notion of *how* THE WORLD is. Any sentence that changes truth-value upon passing from one correct theory to another correct theory – e.g. an equivalent description – will express only a *theory-relative* property of THE WORLD. And the more such sentences there are, the more properties of THE WORLD will turn out to be theory-relative.

For example, if we concede that Story 1 and Story 2 are equivalent descriptions, then the property *being an object* (as opposed to a class or set of things) will be theory-relative. Consider now a third story:

Story 3. *There are only line segments with rational end points* (i.e. since there aren't 'points', in this story, except as logical constructions, (1) every line segment has rational length; (2) the piece of the line[8] between any two line segments is a line segment, and so has rational length; (3) every line segment is divisible into n equal pieces, for every integer n; (4) there is at least one line segment; and (5) the union of two line segments is a line segment). Irrational line segments are treated as logical constructions – sets of 'points', where 'points' are themselves Cauchy convergent sets of *rational* line segments.

A 'hard-core' realist might again object, this time because this story makes an irrational line segment of a different logical type than a rational line segment. But the defender of this story can reply: Isn't it common in mathematics that objects are identified with sets of other objects which are *pre-analytically* of the same logical type? Thus, negative integers and positive integers, whole numbers and rationals, rationals and reals, reals and imaginaries are pre-analytically all 'numbers', but in *formalizing* mathematics we are used to treating negative numbers (or more generally, 'signed numbers') as *ordered pairs* of 'natural numbers', *rational* numbers as *ordered pairs* of 'signed numbers', irrationals as *sets* of rationals, etc. So what is wrong with treating irrational line segments as sets of sets of rational line segments? After all, the rational line segments are a basis for the topology; if you know what is going on in every rational line segment, you have a complete description of all events, etc.

If we accept Story 3 as yet another equivalent description of 'the world', however, then even the *cardinality* of the world becomes theory-relative! For there are only denumberably many objects in Story 3, and non-denumberably many in Stories 1 and 2! (We might try to avoid this by treating *sets* as 'objects', too – but, as I've shown elsewhere, 'set' talk can be translated away into *possibility* talk.)

All this isn't an artifact of my simple example: actual physical theory is rife with similar examples. One can construe space-time points as objects, for example, or as properties. One can construe fields as objects, or do everything with particles acting at a distance (using retarded potentials). The fact is, *so many* properties of THE WORLD – starting with *just* the *categorial* ones, such as cardinality, particulars, or universals, etc. – turn out to be 'theory-relative' that THE WORLD ends up as a Kantian 'noumenal' world, a *mere* 'thing in itself'. If one cannot say *how* THE WORLD is theory-independently, then talk of all these theories as descriptions of 'the world' is empty.

ANOTHER POINT AT WHICH THE METAPHYSICAL REALIST PICTURE RUNS INTO TROUBLE

This has to do with what Quine calls 'ontological relativity'. Suppose we confine attention, for the moment, to *complete* theories. If T is a complete theory, we can define an equivalence relation on its terms – *provable co-extensiveness* – with the property that if two terms belong to different equivalence classes, then in *no* model of the theory do they refer to the same referent, whereas if they belong to the same equivalence class, then they have the same referent in *every* model of the theory. So, for our purposes, we may count terms as the same if they lie in the same equivalence class – i.e. if they are 'co-extensive taking the theory at face value'. With this preliminary identification made, we notice that if our picture is correct – I repeat the picture

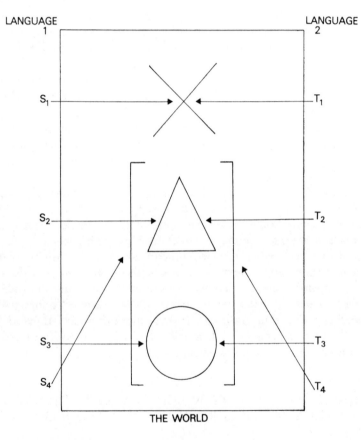

LANGUAGE 1

LANGUAGE 2

S_1 → ← T_1

S_2 → ← T_2

S_3 → ← T_3

S_4 T_4

THE WORLD

– then there is a *unique* reference-preserving 'translation' connecting the Languages.

But it is notorious that there are often *inequivalent* relative interpretations of one theory in another. Story 1 can be interpreted in Story 2 (in the case of our example) in *many* different ways.

'Points' can be sets of line segments whose lengths are negative powers of 2, for example, or sets of line segments whose lengths are negative powers of 3.

If the picture as I drew it were correct, there would have to be a 'fact of the matter' as to *which* translation *really* preserves reference in every such case!

Just as we complicated the picture by allowing the same term to be mapped onto different real objects when it occurs in different theories to meet the previous objection, so we could complicate the picture *again* to meet the second objection: we could say that the language has *more than one* correct way of being mapped onto THE WORLD (it must, since it has more than one way of being correctly mapped onto a language which is *itself* correctly mapped onto the world). But now *all* grasp of the picture seems to vanish: if what is a *unique* set of things *within a correct theory* may not be a unique set of things 'in reality', then the very heart of the picture is torn out.

WHY ALL THIS DOESN'T REFUTE INTERNAL REALISM

Suppose we try to stump the *internal* realist with the question, 'How do you know that "cow" refers to cows?' 'After all', we point out, 'there are other interpretations of your whole language – non-denumerably many interpretations (in the sense of satisfaction-relations), which would render true an *ideal* theory (in your language). Indeed, suppose God gave us the *set of all true sentences* in your language (pretend we have infinite memories, for this purpose). Call this set the *perfect* theory. Then there would *still* be infinitely many admissible interpretations of the *perfect* theory – interpretations which, as we saw, satisfied *all* the operational and theoretical constraints. Even the *sentence* " 'Cow' refers to cows" is true in all of these interpretations. So how do you know that it is true in the sense of being true in a *unique* 'intended' interpretation? How do you know that "cow" refers to cows in the sense of referring to *one* determinate set of things, as opposed to referring to a determinate set of things *in each admissible interpretation*?' (This is, of course, just arguing against the internal realist exactly as we argued against the metaphysical realist.)

The internal realist should reply that '"Cow" refers to cows' follows immediately from the definition of 'refers'. In fact, '"cow" refers to cows' would be true even if internal realism were false: although we can revise '"Cow" refers to cows' by scrapping the theory itself (or at least scrapping or challenging the notion of a *cow*) – and this is how the fact that '"cow" refers to cows' is not *absolutely* unrevisable manifests itself – *relative to the theory*, '"Cow" refers to cows' is a logical truth.

The critic will now reply that his question hasn't been answered. '"Cow" refers to cows' is indeed analytic relative to the theory – but his question challenged *the way the theory is understood*. '"Cow" refers to cows' is true in all admissible interpretations of the theory – but that isn't at issue.

The internal realist should now reply that (1) 'the way the theory is understood' can't be discussed *within* the theory; and (2) the question whether the theory has a *unique* intended interpretation has *no* absolute sense. Viewed from within Story 1 (or a meta-language which contains the object language of Story 1), 'point' has a 'unique intended interpretation'. Viewed from within Story 2 (or a meta-language which contains the object language of Story 2), the term 'point' *as used in Story 1* has a plurality of admissible interpretations. The critic's 'how do you know?' question assumes a theory-independent fact of the matter as to what a term in a given theory corresponds to – i.e. assumes the picture of metaphysical realism; and this is a picture the *internal* realist need not (and better not) accept.

The critic now replies as follows: 'reference' (strictly speaking, 'satisfies') is defined so that

(1) 'Cow' refers to cows

just says (in the case of where 'cow' is a primitive expression of L) that the ordered pair < 'cow', {cows} > belongs to a certain *list* of ordered pairs. If anything, this *presupposes* that 'cow' refers (in some *other* sense of 'refers'); it doesn't *explicate* it.[9]

Answer: the *use* of 'cow' does presuppose that 'cow' is *understood*. And if my account of *understanding* was a *truth-conditional* (or *reference-conditional*) account, then the objection would be good. But I gave a verificationist account of understanding (in terms of degree of confirmation); thus *my use of the term 'cow' in the language* has already been explained, and I am free to use it – even to use it in explaining what 'cow' refers to.

What I am saying is that, in a certain 'contextual' sense, it is an *a priori* truth that 'cow' refers to a determinate class of things (or a more-or-less-determinate class of things – I neglect ordinary vagueness). Adopting 'cow talk' is adopting a 'version', in Nelson Goodman's phrase, from within which it is *a priori* that the word 'cow' refers (and, indeed, that it refers to cows).

One of the puzzling things about the metaphysical realist picture is that it makes it unintelligible how there can *be a priori* truths, even contextual ones, even as a (possibly unreachable) limit. An *a priori* truth would have to be the product of a kind of direct 'intuition' of the things themselves. Even verbal truth is hard to understand. Consider 'all bachelors are unmarried'. It can be 'verbal' that this is in some sense 'short for' 'all unmarried men are unmarried'. And this, in turn, is an instance of 'All AB are A'. But why is *this* true?

Suppose there *were* unrevisability – *absolute* unrevisability. And suppose we held 'All AB are A' (and even 'All unmarried men are unmarried') absolutely immune from revision. Why would this make it *true*?

Suppose, unimaginably, there are some AB that are not A. (After all, there are lots of things in modern science we can't imagine.) Then, on the metaphysical realist picture, our refusal to give up assenting to 'All AB are A' doesn't make *it* true – it just makes *us* stubborn.[10]

Once we abandon the metaphysical realist picture, the situation becomes quite different. Suppose we include a sentence S in the ideal theory T_1 just because it is a feature we *want* the ideal theory to have that it contain S. (Suppose we even hold S 'immune' from revision, as a behaviouristic fact about us.) Assuming S doesn't make T_1 inconsistent, T_1 *still* has a model. And since the model isn't fixed *independently* of the theory, T_1 will be *true* – true in *the* model (from the point of view of *meta*-T_1); true in all *admissible* models, from the point of view of a theory in which the terms of T_1 do not determinately refer to begin with. So S will be true! 'S' is 'analytic' – but it is an 'analyticity' that resembles Kant's account of the *synthetic a priori* more than it resembles his account of the analytic. For the 'analytic' sentence is, so to speak, part of 'the form of the representation' and not 'the content of the representation'. It can't be false of the world (as opposed to THE WORLD), because the world is not describable independently of our description.

Even if T_1 were *inconsistent* if we were consistently inconsistent (assigned 'truth' and 'falsity' to sentences in a stable way), this would not block this argument: for *stable* inconsistency can be viewed as *reinterpretation of the logical connectives*. When we give up the metaphysical realist picture we see for the first time how a truth can be 'about the world' ('All AB are A' *is* 'about the world' – it is about all *classes* A, B) and 'without content'.

In the foregoing, I used the idea of an absolutely 'unrevisable' truth as an idealization. Of course, I agree with Quine that this is an unattainable 'limit'. Any statement can be 'revised'. But what is often overlooked, although Quine stresses it again and again, is that the revisability of the laws of Euclid's geometry, or the laws of classical logic, does not make them mere 'empirical' statements. This is why I have called them *contextually a priori*.[11] Quine put the point very well when he said that 'the lore of our fathers' is black with fact and white with convention, and added that there are no *completely* white threads and no quite black ones. One might describe this as a soft (and demythologized) Kantianism. A trouble with the metaphysical realist picture is that one cannot see how there can be white at all – even greyish white.

Let me close with a last philosophical metaphor. Kant's image was of knowledge as a 'representation' – a kind of play. The author is me. But the author also appears as a character in the play (like a Pirandello play). The author in the play is not the 'real' author – it is the 'empirical me'. The 'real' author is the 'transcendental me'.

I would modify Kant's image in two ways. The authors (in the plural – my image of knowledge is social) don't write just *one* story: they write many versions. And the authors *in* the stories are the *real* authors. This would be 'crazy' if these stories were *fictions*. A fictitious character can't also be a real author. But these are true stories.

NOTES

1 This is spelled out in my 'What is "Realism"?', in *Proceedings of the Aristotelian Society* (1975–6), pp. 177–94. Part I, Lecture II of this volume.
2 Delivered in Jerusalem, May 1976, Part III of this volume.
3 If THE WORLD is finite, let the theory be compatible with there being only N individuals (where N is the cardinality of THE WORLD), and pick a model with N individuals instead of using the stronger model-theoretic theorem appealed to in the text.
4 Here, if SAT is a relation of the same logical type as 'satisfies', TRUE(SAT) is supposed to be defined in terms of SAT exactly as 'true' is defined in terms of 'satisfies' (by Tarski). Thus 'TRUE(SAT)' is the truth-property 'determined' by the relation SAT.
5 This is most completely spelled out in his (unpublished) William James Lectures. A partial account appears in his contribution to the conference on 'Language, Intentionality, and Translation Talk' reprinted in *Synthese*, vol. 27, nos 3/4 (July/August, 1974).
6 Cf. my 'The Meaning of "Meaning"' in my *Mind, Language, and Reality; Philosophical Papers*, vol. 2, Cambridge University Press, 1975.
7 Compare the alternative systems discussed in Nelson Goodman, *The Structure of Appearance*, Reidel, Dordrecht, 1951, 1977, ch. 1, sections 1–4.
8 The mathematical reader will note that in Story 3 there is no distinction between *open* and *closed* line segments – because there are no such things as *points*!
9 This objection to Tarskian definitions of reference is due to Hartry Field (cf. his 'Tarski's Theory of Truth', *Journal of Philosophy*, vol. 69, no. 13 (1972), pp. 347–75) and is discussed in my John Locke Lectures (Part I of this book).
10 The reader may be tempted to reply that even a metaphysical realist is entitled to the notion of a *verbal convention*. And why can't it be a verbal *convention* that no state of affairs is to be referred to as the *conjunction* of the states of affairs described by sentences *p, q* unless it entails both

p and *q* separately? This would mean that '*p·q* entails *p*' is 'true by convention'; and similarly, 'All AB are A' could be 'true by convention'.

The difficulty is that such a 'convention' only makes it analytic that the conjunction *p·q* entails *p* *if the state of affairs in question exists*. But how can the *existence* of a state of affairs with the properties of entailing *p* and entailing *q* and being entailed by every state of affairs which entails both *p* and *q* be *itself* a matter of *convention*, on the metaphysical realist picture?

To establish that this is not trifling, let me remark that there are logics (studied by David Finkelstein in connection with certain 'far out' physical theories – *not* standard quantum theory) in which (1) there are propositions *incompatible* with any given proposition; but (2) there is no such thing as *the* negation of a given proposition —i.e. no logically weakest proposition incompatible with a given proposition. (These logics correspond algebraically to lattices which are not orthocomplemented.) If 'the logic of the world' is one of *these* logics (as Finkelstein believes), then *the existence of a complement* to a given state of affairs is *false as a matter of fact* – and *no* linguistic convention *could* render it true!

It seems to me that a consistent metaphysical realist must *either* view logic as empirical, not just in the sense of thinking that logic is revisable (which I believe), but in the sense of having *no* conventional component at all (so that even our confidence that statements aren't *both* true and false becomes ultimately just *inductive* confidence), *or* he must believe that logic is *a priori* in a sense of *a priori* which is not explainable by the notion of convention at all.

11 In 'It Ain't Necessarily So', reprinted in my *Mind, Language and Reality; Philosophical Papers,* vol. 2, Cambridge University Press, 1975.

Index

INDEX

INDEX

linguistic: behaviour, 40, 100–3, 105–6, 108, 112, 116; competence, 129; division of labour, 98, 114

literature, 5, 83, 85–9, 94; as source of knowledge, 89–92 logic, 35, 46, 73, 75; classical, 26–30, 34, 36, 46, 108, 128, 138; deductive, 15, 98, 102, 107–8, 112, 115; inductive, 12, 67, 70–1, 98, 105, 108, 112, 115; non-classical, 25–7

logical: connectives, 12, 25–31, 34, 36–7, 108, 112, 138; empiricism, 36, 66, 70

McDowell, John, 74, 98

Mach, Ernst, 112

Mailer, Norman, 88

Marx, Marxism, 59

mathematical intuitionism, *see* intuitionism

mathematics, 2, 132–3; in social science, 59

meaning, 10, 37–9, 41–2, 44, 47, 69–71, 100, 110, 113, 115–17, 129; change, 99, 114–15; 'museum myth', 49–50; picture theory, 97, 100; probability theory, 111–14; and realism, 113–14; and use, 3, 97, 99, 112, 117, 127; *see also* language use

Mendel, Gregor, 22

meta-language, 2–3, 10–11, 16, 28, 31, 48, 107, 111, 128–9, 136; with infinite conjunctions and disjunctions, 15

metaphysical realism, 6, 123–30, 132–3, 137–8

metaphysics, 1–2, 9–10, 48, 75, 92, 94, 101–3, 107

might-statements, 109

Mill, J. S., 5, 66–7, 69

Minsky, Marvin, 57

Moore, G. E., 108

moral philosophy, 5, 83–7, 92–4

moral sciences, 5, 66

Murdoch, Iris, 59

Murisaki, Lady, 86

Nagel, Ernest, 66–9, 75

Newton, Isaac, 19, 22

object language, 2–3, 10–11, 15–16, 28, 99, 111, 136

objectivity, 76, 84–5, 93, 125

observables/unobservables, 29, 111–12; macro-, 99

observation sentences, 20–1, 27, 35–6, 125

Occam, William, 126

ontological relativity, 133

operationalism, 18, 21, 56, 90, 125–6

Peirce, C. S., 1, 36, 125

perception, 35, 103, 110; visual, 103–5, 108; *see also* observables

phenomenalism, 36, 102, 111, 113, 128

physicalism, 4, 14–15, 17, 32–3, 38, 41, 59, 61, 64

physics, 21, 60–2, 72, 92; compared with moral sciences, 5, 66; compared with social sciences, 51, 53, 59, 62, 65, 66–8, 73, 75–7

Pike, Kenneth, 55–6

Platonism, 66, 75, 93

plausibility, 75, 90–1, 125

Polanyi, M., 73

Popper, Karl, 3, 75

positivism, 1, 18–20, 73, 102

possibility, 35, 63–4, 75, 108, 133

pragmatism, 2, 42, 47, 102, 126

prediction, 17, 19–22, 27, 30, 43, 63–4, 67, 102

primitive (undefined) notions, reference, etc., 2, 10–11, 14–16, 28, 32; list, 11–12, 16, 30–1

principle, *see* 'in principle' concept

probability, 2–3, 9, 35, 40, 98, 111–12; prior, 75, 105

propositional calculus, 26–7

Protagoras, 30

provability, 2, 26–9, 34, 36, 46, 128

psychology, 41–3, 46–54, 56, 59, 62, 71–5, 85, 87, 89, 92, 105

quasi-intuitionism, *see* intuitionism

Quine, W. V., vii–ix, 9, 17, 23, 32, 37, 40–1, 44–5, 49–51, 53, 58, 69–70, 133, 138

Rawls, John, 84

real time, 64–5

realism, 29, 50–1, 100, 102, 107–8, 112–14, 116, 130–2; empirical, 4–5, 19, 123, 130; and idealism, 9, 18, 37–8, 106, 108–9, 111; internal, 123, 125, 128, 130, 135–6; metaphysical, 6, 123–30, 132, 137–8; and science,

143

International Library of Philosophy & Scientific Method

Editor: Ted Honderich

(Demy 8vo)

Allen, R. E. (Ed.), **Studies in Plato's Metaphysics** *464 pp. 1965.*
  Plato's 'Euthyphro' and the Earlier Theory of Forms *184 pp. 1970.*
Allen, R. E. and Furley, David J. (Eds.), **Studies in Presocratic Philosophy**
  Volume II *448 pp. 1975.*
Armstrong, D. M., **Perception and the Physical World** *208 pp. 1961.*
  A Materialist Theory of the Mind *376 pp. 1967.*
Bambrough, Renford (Ed.), **New Essays on Plato and Aristotle**
  184 pp. 1965.
Barry, Brian, **Political Argument** *382 pp. 1965.*
Bird, Graham, **Kant's Theory of Knowledge** *220 pp. 1962.*
Bogen, James, **Wittgenstein's Philosophy of Language** *256 pp. 1972.*
Broad, C. D., **Lectures on Psychical Research** *461 pp. 1962.*
  (2nd Impression 1966.)
Crombie, I. M., **An Examination of Plato's Doctrine**
  I. Plato on Man and Society *408 pp. 1962.*
  II. Plato on Knowledge and Reality *583 pp. 1963.*
Day, John Patrick, **Inductive Probability** *352 pp. 1961.*
Dennett, D. C., **Content and Consciousness** *202 pp. 1969.*
Dretske, Fred I., **Seeing and Knowing** *270 pp. 1969.*
Ducasse, C. J., **Truth, Knowledge and Causation** *263 pp. 1969.*
Edel, Abraham, **Method in Ethical Theory** *379 pp. 1963.*
Farm, K. T. (Ed.), **Symposium on J. L. Austin** *512 pp. 1969.*
Findlay, J. N., **Plato: The Written and Unwritten Doctrines** *498 pp. 1974.*
Flew, Anthony, **Hume's Philosophy of Belief** *296 pp. 1961.*
Fogelin, Robert J., **Evidence and Meaning** *200 pp. 1967.*
Franklin, R., **Freewill and Determinism** *353 pp. 1968.*
Furley, David J. and Allen, R. E. (Eds.), **Studies in Presocratic Philosophy**
  Volume I *326 pp. 1970.*
Gale, Richard, **The Language of Time** *256 pp. 1967.*
Glover, Jonathan, **Responsibility** *212 pp. 1970.*
Goldman, Lucien, **The Hidden God** *424 pp. 1964.*
Hamlyn, D. W., **Sensation and Perception** *222 pp. 1961.*
  (3rd Impression 1967.)
Husserl, Edmund, **Logical Investigations** *Vol. I : 456 pp. Vol. II : 464 pp.*
Kemp, J., **Reason, Action and Morality** *216 pp. 1964.*
Körner, Stephan, **Experience and Theory** *272 pp. 1966.*
Lazerowitz, Morris, **Studies in Metaphilosophy** *276 pp. 1964.*
Linsky, Leonard, **Referring** *152 pp. 1967.*
Mackenzie, Brian D., **The Origins of Behaviourism,** *1976.*
MacIntosh, J. J. and Coval, S. C. (Eds.), **Business of Reason** *280 pp. 1969.*
Meiland, Jack W., **Talking About Particulars** *192 pp. 1970.*
Merleau-Ponty, M., **Phenomenology of Perception** *487 pp. 1962.*
Naess, Arne, **Scepticism** *176 pp. 1969.*
Perelman, Chaim, **The Idea of Justice and the Problem of Argument**
  224 pp. 1963.
Rorty, A. (Ed.), **Personal Identity** *1975.*